Boy in a Slouch Hat

First published in Australia in 2014 by Ted George
1 Irwin Place, Maida Vale, WA 6057
slouch.hat@westnet.com.au

© Ted George, 2014
All rights reserved. No part of this book may be reproduced or transmitted in any form or by any means, electronic or mechanical, including photocopying, recording or by any information storage and retrieval system, without prior permission in writing from the publisher.

National Library of Australia
Cataloguing-in-Publication entry:

George, Ted, 1947–
Boy in a slouch hat: before, during and after Vietnam / Ted George
1st ed.
ISBN: 9780646908267 (paperback)
George, Ted, author.

George, Ted—Childhood and youth.
Vietnam War, 1961–1975—Personal narratives, Australian.
Soldiers—Australia—Biography.
Men—Biography.
Australia—Armed Forces—Biography.

959.7043092

Consultant editor: Georgia Richter, ProofEd Editing Services
Editor: Leila Jabour
Design and typeset: Carolyn Brown, furrylogic
Printed by Lightning Source, Victoria

Boy in a Slouch Hat

Before, During and After Vietnam

TED GEORGE

In Memory of Old Maida Vale

Contents

Prologue	1
Before	7
During	51
After	115
Glossary	218
The eighteenth green	220

Prologue

The old dog

The old dog stared at the trunk of the lilac tree and nothing happened. He felt nothing and smelt nothing. His tired legs lowered him to the ground; they could do little else. He lay there, one eye crusted with sand, the other staring at the trunk of the lilac tree. He was beyond worry, unknowingly content that he was a picture in time.

Warmth gathered behind his eyes like morphine to a soldier. The radio on the window ledge of the veterans' hospital was tuned in to the horseracing station, but the old dog heard nothing as the warmth behind his eyes took over one more sense. Numbness gave him a warm feeling all over, and the things he felt were all in his mind. As a soldier has phantom pain where there is no limb, an old dog has phantom comfort, warmth and security where there is none.

The sheets and pillowcases are crisp and clean, as is the air coming in through the normally closed window. A nurse slams the window shut and pushes the medicine trolley towards my bed. A jab in the arm and I can see halfway to the shiny white ceiling, where I read these words that are drifting towards the now-closed window: 'Loneliness is a dead dog's breakfast.'

Hollywood Hospital

The day doctor down in Vung Tau, who I think was in charge of minor surgery, had stitched my left foot back together so I could fly back to Perth, where I was now waiting for a surgeon to open it up again and reconnect the tendons and nerves that had been severed.

G Ward in Perth's Hollywood Repatriation Hospital was bearable because I was alive, pain-free and mostly intact. A familiar warm buzzing inside my head helped me to avoid concern as I lay in my hospital bed waiting for the surgeon: I was removed from the people around me and from my circumstances, over which I had no control.

After many days and nights spent staring at the glossy white ceiling, a familiar face that I would rather not have seen again appeared at the end of my bed. The doctor who had done the first operation on my foot in Vung Tau stood there and told me he would be performing the second 'and hopefully final' operation.

I felt no comfort in his saying 'hopefully', or in seeing him at all. Although he was a major, he was not one of the highly respected surgeons who operated in the Vung Tau hospital; his rank did not reflect his skill. Two young captains who I presumed were still back in Vietnam were known to be the top surgeons, and I wished they were there at the end of my bed.

When you're in a hospital bed, especially in a military repatriation hospital like Hollywood, patients come and go—some head first, some feet first. Night-time coughing and snoring gives way to daytime coughing and smoking; visitors in their Sunday clothes come and go. Your mind travels with them, roaming far and wide, looking to make sense of life.

When I was twelve years old I looked down the barrel of a Lee Enfield .303. I'd wanted to see if the firing pin would move when I pulled the trigger, but I couldn't reach it. Just as well, really, because there was a bullet in the way. That same year, when I was building a flying fox out of old fencing wire, the wire snapped and wrapped itself around my neck, then tightened around my neck until it snapped again and I fell onto a small lucerne tree and slid all the way down the trunk with pencil-thin branches breaking against my legs, causing pain but not slowing my descent.

Yes, I should have died several times before I was conscripted into the army.

If I'd been a Christian I would have thought it was God looking out for me, but that wasn't the case: lying there in hospital I couldn't make that leap of faith. I do believe now that someone has been looking out for me—and that perhaps there is a God, and that maybe one day I'll even understand what it's all about—but back then I just couldn't understand why people kept telling me they would pray for me and, in particular, for the young man—no, boy—in the bed opposite.

He was a brave person with a big smile and a red face. When our visitors had left we would talk quietly, sharing our concerns about the diminishing buzz of immortality. We told stories, too. He'd only been in Vietnam three weeks when he was blown up. His relatives, particularly the older ones, had red faces too, but they were too old to have the buzz and the lines showed on their faces.

I believe that my chances of survival have always been good. Bravery has never been my strong point, but I believe that a person who has brave thoughts has a fair chance of controlling their emotions. It's part bluff, of course, but it keeps your cheeks warm and it protects your eyes from penetrating the fear that's hiding all around you.

Mr. Arthur E. Gouge,

Dampier Mining,

KOOLAN ISLAND, W. A., 6733.

Registration No. 5019765

Before

CALL-UP

You are hereby called u[p]
Military Forces of the Commonwea[lth]

You are required to pr[esent]

[...] Call Up Notice, Certi[ficate]

This notice should be [...]
Certificate of Registration pres[ented]

Enclosed are travel warran[ts]
your journey from Koolan Island to [...]
finally, from Derby to Perth. Bec[ause]
will depart Koolan Island at 7.30 [...]
will travel to Port Hedland by MMA [...]
1968. At Port Hedland you will depa[rt at]
12.45 p.m. on 1st October, 1968. On [...]
the warrants you will be supplied wi[th]

Hang on for the ride

One of my earliest childhood memories of fear and bravery happened at the annual Perth Royal Show, which was held just down the road from the hospital window I later found myself staring out of. Heading west from Hollywood Hospital, the road takes you past Karrakatta Cemetery, the old 'mental hospital', the army barracks and then on to the Claremont Showgrounds. As far as I can remember, that's where my journey started.

My father, a machinery engineer, was looking after me while working at the Show—a duty he was not completely happy with. My mother and three older sisters were off gallivanting around the Show, eating fairy floss, visiting all the food halls and going down to Sideshow Alley and winning dolls and toys—and some good things, too, like water pistols. Every now and then they would come back to the machinery shed and show me what they'd won.

It was all new to me—especially my dad looking after me. At one point he said to me, 'Let's go for a walk and have a look at the animals,' and the next thing I knew I was sitting on an elephant.

My hands were tightly gripping the front handrail of the riding rack, my feet were sticking through the frame and bravely touching the top of the elephant's head, and my father was saying, 'Hang on for the ride.'

From where I was sitting I could see further than I had

ever seen before, and as this huge animal moved slowly around the showgrounds, I marvelled at my own movement without effort. Looking down from this high place I saw the tops of people's heads, most wearing hats, and a lot of ladies with bright sun umbrellas. Everyone seemed to be having a happy time.

There were a few other kids on this ride, all older than me, but I got to sit at the front in the middle. I'm not sure whether my dad knew the fellow who ran the ride or whether he'd slipped something extra into his hand when the owner said I was a bit young for an elephant ride.

Afterwards, Dad carried me back to the machinery shed, stopping on the way to have a photo taken of me with a screaming white cocky on my shoulder. These were both good but somewhat scary experiences.

Back at the shed, Dad, a proud man, introduced me to his old army sergeant who had dropped in to say hello. The two of them smiled at each other with red faces, shook hands several times and repeated each other's name just as often, before the sergeant left and disappeared into the crowd. The other men who worked with Dad were testing motors and pumps. They were all dressed in suits and ties and had white faces and were busy explaining to farmers and miners how their machinery worked.

Space was tight at the showgrounds, and the sheds were so close together that a small boy could just fit between them, lean his back against one shed wall, push one leg straight out in front of him to support himself against the opposite wall, shimmy a little, then lift the other leg a little higher and brace it there. Using this method he could climb to the top of the sheds, which were very high, from where he could see the whole showgrounds.

I remember the smell of new paint from the heated machinery, the noise, and the food, like showground chocolate—yes, that chocolate was the best.

But mostly I remember my father's words: 'Hang on for the ride.'

An hour at six

Well, it was an ordinary day. I was about six years old and dressed in my Robin Hood outfit. Mum's friend, Mrs Wilson, who was an excellent cook, was looking after me for the afternoon. I could see the outline of the city but it was very quiet where I was standing on the well-used grass driveway running down the side of Mr and Mrs Wilson's house. Mr Wilson worked for Dunlop and knew all there was to know about tyres.

A perfect morning temperature, the sun was friendly; there was an old garage to the back, and a quiet road to the front. I was all alone. I didn't know which way to go. I didn't know where Mrs Wilson was. I stood there, content, until I thought perhaps I was in the wrong place and someone might see me.

Three ants crossed the track heading for the shade under the house. I stood motionless as they passed in front of my toes. I thought they must not have seen me or they wouldn't have been so brave. I was one with nature.

The sun and silence echoed warm feelings. I thought that if I flapped my arms I could fly. So I flapped my arms slowly, but only briefly, for fear of ridicule. I had four sisters. I didn't want to face the possibility that no matter how fast I flapped I might not take off.

I learned that there is security in knowledge, and safety in caution.

The corner shop

The ants disappeared under the house. I didn't quite take off and I didn't need to think about where I was. Nature was on my side. I headed for the road and turned left towards the corner shop.

I had to cross the road to get to the shop—the road where only weeks before Ronny Wilson had tested his dad's theory that truck tyres are made out of soft rubber. He's all right now, of course, but that theory and his courage earned my respect.

The sun was shining onto the shop window and the half-metal flywire door, reflecting heat onto the footpath. Surely this couldn't be the same sun that had been my friend in the grass driveway?

I looked in through the window. Mr and Mrs Coin didn't look happy now that they were working for the shearer who'd won the shop from them in a poker game. Ants were a problem, there was no air conditioning and the bread was yesterday's, but I was in a safe environment, and if I kept moving, no one was going to say I shouldn't be there.

Anyway, the thing about not liking where you are is that at least you can say in your defence that you don't like where you are, that whatever happens it's not your fault if you're not there of your own free will—especially if someone has dressed you in a funny way and made you carry a sword.

I went back to Mrs Wilson's and sat on the back steps

watching her taking down the washing. It was cool in the shade. I felt again at one with my surroundings, even though I knew she would probably want me to move when she brought the washing into the house. My uncluttered brain thought there must be a place where there are steps just for sitting on.

Big kids and their dads

Tom's dad was also named Tom. They were a nice family, the Hugalls. They had a chook farm. Tom Sr wore an old grey dustcoat, short pants, and army boots that he never laced up properly. He collected eggs in a wheelbarrow.

Tom Jr played footy with Tim Marshall—another nice family, the Marshalls. Tim's dad drove a shiny white car and wore long white socks. He had a small neat white moustache and he was called Mr Marshall.

My dad had a small white moustache too. It covered up a wound from a Japanese hand grenade. Dad had lots of friends who came to visit, and the one thing they all had in common was that they had all gone to war to serve their country. They would sit down and put their hats on our glass coffee table. They all wore RSL badges on their lapels and their faces shone in each other's company: this was apparent even to a small boy sitting quietly behind the couch hoping not to be noticed. War stories sounded exciting—death, of course, was no more real than in a comic book.

In those days, with World War II still fresh in the minds of veterans, judgements came easily. You were either from a nice family or you came from a family where the dad had stayed home during the war and made what was called 'easy money'—like the two brothers up the road, who had a trucking business. They'd made so much money that they'd built two big brick houses and sent their sons to the private boys' grammar school.

My first scary adventure away from home was when I started school. Mum had bought me some brand new clothes for school, and underpants, which I had never worn before. They looked like nappies to me, and I knew just the tree to hide them in on the way to school.

When I got to school that first day—having walked the mile from our house in Maida Vale along Cyril and Kalamunda roads to the primary school at the bottom of Kalamunda hill—I couldn't help but notice that a few of the kids were wearing shoes. I wondered whether they'd had to wear underpants as well. I felt as though I'd entered a new world—one where I was expected to dress and be like everyone else.

One of the great freedoms in life is a pee in the bush, or a crap from high up a gum tree on a hot day with a cool breeze. This did not go down well at school. You might say it got me off to a bad start.

With 100°F temperatures in the lunch shed, the smell of hot soft banana in my lunch bag that I can still smell to this day, and four sisters who just loved our new inside toilet, I couldn't think of much to look forward to. I did like Tom and Tim, who were my older sisters' friends. But I was glad I was just a little kid—and from a good family.

Clear blue

I didn't always used to be famous.

I can remember when I was only eight, thinking, 'One more year, and then I can say that next year I'll be ten, and life will be a little clearer.' It's remarkable that things were so clear at eight. I can remember staring at a crystal-clear blue sky while riding our horse in the shade of some silver clouds with dark-grey bottoms. As the clouds passed, I stopped Dear John, crossed my legs over his mane, lay back with my head on his rump and looked straight through that crystal blue sky, through one universe to the next. After some time I reached infinity and achieved a feeling of great security.

Then Dear John, on his own initiative, walked under a low branch and knocked me off. After the fall, things remained just as distinct but somehow a bit more important as I sat in the double-gee patch. Dear John knew where those prickles were.

Everything seemed so well defined, as if staring into the blue had given me magnifying glasses: the passionfruit vines growing up the lucerne trees; our house only a stone's throw away; and the two really big apricot trees with new green fruit that would keep us busy at harvest time, picking, washing and preserving laundry baskets full of fruit. I was surrounded by a mixed orchard of peaches, plums and figs. Big-leafed grape vines clung to anything to get themselves off the ground. Our lemons, oranges and mandarins seemed to fruit all year round, but our apricots were the best in town. There were some who thought the fact that they grew next to the septic tank might have had something to do with it.

I unbridled Dear John and walked the stone's throw to our house and up its two steps, went inside and closed the flywire door behind me before Dear John could stick his nose in and hold it open. He had a habit of doing that. He loved human contact, as long as you didn't put a saddle on him or make him walk or run too far. Sometimes, a few of us kids would ride him at once: six was the record. That lasted as long as it took Dear John to find a low branch and wipe us all off.

Dear John

One day when all of us kids were at school, Dear John followed Mum inside when she brought in a basket of washing. Her hands were full; she couldn't close the door. Dear John followed her up the steps, through the door, across the back veranda, up the step to the hallway, down the short hallway and into the kitchen. Only then did Mum realise that this great big horse was right behind her.

She was worried he would go through the floorboards, so she just wanted him to stay still until we got home from school. Well, Dear John must have liked it where he was, because he didn't move. Mum did the cooking and the ironing, all under Dear John's nose, and they seemed to build up some sort of rapport that afternoon.

When we got home from school and saw Dear John in the kitchen—well, speaking for myself, I felt that I matured a little right then, as I took on an air of confidence I hadn't known I had and said, 'It's all right, Mum, we can take care of this.'

Mum had a concerned sort of smile on her face, but we got Dear John to turn around in the kitchen and Sue, my little sister, led him out. We all felt kind of clever—especially Dear John, who had finally made it into the kitchen.

The following Sunday we were all sitting down to our traditional roast lunch of two big golden-brown chickens with lots of roasted vegetables and some greens. There were eight of us in the family—not counting Dear John. Bet was the oldest, then Trish, Nona, me, Sue and Jenny, plus Mum and Dad.

(There was also Spotty the dog, but he was strictly Sue's dog. He was a stray that she'd brought home one day. Mum had told me to get a rope and tow him somewhere on my bike. I'd done this, and about a mile away I'd let him go and he'd taken off through the bush. By the time I'd got home Spotty had caught his breath and was having a lie-down in the sun under the lilac tree. We had Spotty for about four years when Mr Richards, the farmer-butcher from down the road, shot him dead for chasing his sheep.)

Our Sunday roast lunch was an important family time. I learned about life, loyalty and fairness there. I can still see the two big roast chooks and all the roast vegies, and the two large old-fashioned glass bottles of Coca-Cola from which Bet and Trish measured out equal glasses under our watchful eyes. It was a formal occasion, with a tablecloth, placemats and the good silver.

The kitchen table ran alongside a row of louvred windows without flywire screens. On this particular Sunday, after the main course when we were enjoying Mum's preserved apricots and Dad's homemade vanilla ice-cream, Dear John came up to the window, turned his head sideways and stuck his nose through the glass louvres. I gave him a sugar cube, but something must have scared him because he lifted his head and broke two of the louvres. After that, Dad decided to build a fence between the house and the back five acres. The horse was not impressed.

Dear John didn't like leaving the property. The best he would do was a trot on leaving. I think he knew a trot was uncomfortable for the rider, especially bareback and not wearing any underpants. It makes my eyes water just thinking about it.

On the way home he would canter, and that was fun—even though he was in complete control. It was fast and easy riding. You could let go of the reins—you could even turn around backwards. He was heading home and that's all there was to it. Riding was over for the day.

Brave arc

I walked down our sandy horse trail, aimlessly looking for adventure or someone to play with, but my footprints were at odds with all the animal prints. A willy wagtail and a magpie, intent on arguing, didn't even notice me. I could have caught them both—that would've taught them that horses, snakes and lizards weren't the only ones that used that trail.

Thick bushes bordered the hot sandy track and the sun was uncomfortable on my back. My shorts with their failing elastic barely hung on. I hadn't pulled them up in a long time, and there could only be a step or two before it would be too late, but caring about that could not erode the boredom of an eight-year-old boy as he passed through the bush. And so, feeling that I was the first person ever to be where I was, I let my pants fall to the sand, stepped out of them, and ran naked through the bush.

Casting caution aside, I even hurdled over blackboy bushes. I felt almost as if I could fly, as I travelled in a subconscious arc that would return me to my pants. It was a bit of a dare to myself—a sort of bravery test.

On my way through the bush I came upon the McLartys' boundary fence, from where I could see their fine brick house. Lenna McLarty, who was two years and seven months older than me and who I called Lenna McFarty, lived there. The best swimming hole in the whole creek was just inside their boundary fence, and just out of sight of their house.

In silence I jumped the barbed-wire fence, tumble-rolled across the sandy firebreak, ran the few paces to the creek and, with a Tarzan-like yell, jumped as high as I could, making the biggest splash possible as I hit the water. I then scrambled back through the fence as quickly as I could and ran flat-out to my pants, which were waiting for me in the sand.

My naked journey had been short in duration but long in bravery and accomplishment. The dare was over.

Still with a thirst for adventure, but now with my clothes back on, I climbed a tree from where I could see the main road. The morning traffic had already passed, and there probably wouldn't be another car until late afternoon, unless someone came home early. So I imagined a fire engine turning up our rough corrugated gravel road and stopping in front of our house, the gravel turning to the red dust of the outback country where I was born, and Stan the fire-engine driver jumping out of the truck's cabin, his knees buckling slightly as he landed on the hard red earth.

That sure would be an exciting job all right—carrying an axe, wearing a helmet, squirting a big fire hose and, most of all, not having to walk everywhere.

In my fertile imagination, Stan looked at the water bag that was hanging from the roo bar and sighed. Tired and dirty, he removed his sunglasses as the sweat dripped down his cheeks, splashing onto the red dust.

Best memory

When I was eight the early-morning sun shone through our apricot tree and in through my louvred window, warming my bedroom floor. The narrow rays highlighted particles of dust in motion, and when I kicked back my blanket more dust appeared in the strips of sunlight. Some of the particles were travelling in opposite directions, as if they were self-propelled and had somewhere to go.

Staring at this early-morning complexity was simple and easy to do, and very little thought was required. The sun was up and there was warmth in the Saturday-morning air. The stuff that was going to happen had already happened: all the cars had gone to work, the dogs had stopped barking and were resting in the shade of the water tank, the windmill was still and the house was quiet—except for an alarming 'drip, drip, drip' sound coming from the kitchen. Bedtime was over: action was required.

After turning off the kitchen tap, I noticed a small door key under the draining board. There was only one door that was ever locked in our house, so it must be Dad's wardrobe key.

The key opened his wardrobe, and I proudly put on his army jacket and slouch hat and stared at the black metal barrel of his war rifle leaning against the back of the wardrobe between the suit jackets and ties. I dared not touch it. I returned the jacket and hat, locked the door, replaced the key and ran.

The creek was not far away. 'To the creek!' I yelled. 'To the creek! To the creek-creek-creek!'

A slow fish in the morning sun made a bubble that took forever to form from the side of its mouth. The bubble was reluctant to let go, and the fish, not needing the air, toyed with its size. It was modestly in control, and did not claim to be clever—no, that would have required responsibility, and the fish didn't look like it wanted any of that. Looking cross-eyed, and with its mind concentrating solely on the bubble, it let it go. The bubble headed for the surface of the creek in a wobbly manner and the fish, with a wiggle of its tail, headed for the cooler deeper water.

The noises at the creek were always the same. Birds whistled and squawked, dry leaves rustled under a goanna, and when a roo spotted me running it bounded off through the bush with contemptuous speed. I sat down on the bank for a while and wondered whether my being there made any difference to anything else—and, more concerning, whether I was a part of what was going on, and if so, whether I was an important part. Then I started thinking about food, as I often did when things got too complicated.

It took about twenty minutes to run from Newburn Road Creek to my place, and as I ran I wondered what it would be like to starve to death, like some kids had in a book I'd read at school.

I'd been running for about ten minutes, and nothing out of the ordinary had happened. I'd trod on one goanna, seen two emus and surprised that speedy roo who was resting in the shade of a blackboy bush. When I reached the downhill part of Newburn Road, I stopped for a rest and walked for a bit. I wasn't puffed or anything, I was just having a bit of a think about life. That's where I was when a big truck pulled up and unloaded a massive bulldozer. Then a car pulled up next to it and two men wearing long white socks got out. They rolled out a big piece of paper and spread it out on the bonnet of the car, showing it to the bulldozer driver, who was wearing boots and short socks.

I raced home to tell Mum, hurdling through the untouched bush in the shade of huge trees, the swamp and then the small natural gravel pit that sometimes filled with water.

When I reached Cyril Road I saw two more workmen, who were putting up a big metal sign with a strange name on it on the side of our gravel road, saying we were going to be a new suburb with brick houses, sealed roads and mains water.

In the following weeks the bulldozer worked eight hours a day, pushing down trees and bush and making huge piles that the driver then set fire to, covering Maida Vale in smoke.

Long white socks

Those men in long white socks who had paid the bulldozer operator to knock down all the trees and change the name of where I grew up were the same men who later paid for the creek to be put into big concrete pipes.

Those men in long white socks, Mum said, call themselves developers. Mum had tried to stop them from knocking down all the trees. Coming from the goldfields, she knew the importance of trees. She'd stood in front of a big jarrah tree across the road from our house, and when the bulldozer man had come to knock it down she'd refused to move. He'd known he wasn't going to win an argument with a woman like that, so he'd moved on to all the other tress and flattened the whole area.

My mum always knew what was right and wrong, and she wasn't afraid to say so. The speed limit in the metro area was thirty-five miles an hour then, and one day when Mum was driving to town in the Humber Super Snipe, a policeman on a motorbike—who Mum said was doing no more than thirty-four miles an hour—was painfully holding up her progress. After some miles had passed, Mum had had enough of this smart aleck so she slowly passed him, going about thirty-eight miles an hour.

The morning after Mum had stood in front of that big jarrah tree across the road, before breakfast, we heard a loud roaring motor and a tremendous crack as the taproot of that jarrah tree snapped under the immense pressure of the bulldozer's push bar and the big tree crashed to the ground. That was the last we saw of the bulldozer and its driver. His work was done, and he was on his way. He could never return to where I grew up. It didn't exist anymore.

When all the new little brick houses were built it was hard to remember the trees and the bulldozer. When the mains water was put on I forgot about the creek for a while. We could have longer showers, and the sewerage system was a good idea, I have to admit—although during the first heavy rain our whole front yard flooded. That was fun, but they were the only good things.

When the new people moved into the little brick houses and built fences and grew lawns, we couldn't ride our horse there anymore. The bush was all gone. The kangaroos, the emus and the goannas all left, and I don't know where they went.

My mum was great. She was brave and kind, and in moments of turmoil her skin stayed soft and cool. She was great, my mum, and that was probably the most important thing when I was eight.

The man in charge

The Christmas holidays I was twelve years old and had started to grow hair in my armpits, my cousin Sonsie and her girlfriend were twenty years old and my grandmother was three hundred and twenty-six—a remarkable woman for her age. She was still working as the chief cook at the Wembley Hotel when she took up her granddaughter's invitation to take a trip to Mount Magnet to visit her daughter and the other grandchildren.

A trip from Perth to Mount Magnet in 1959 was a modest venture compared to the journeys our forefathers had taken in their search for gold—some in Model T Fords, some on pushbikes and some pushing wheelbarrows with metal wheels along the sandy and corrugated gravel roads.

I was a late inclusion in my cousin's travel plans, making four of us in an old four-cylinder Hillman that you had to change down a gear going up the smallest of hills. It was a full load with four people, a water drum and food stacked in the middle of the back seat, plus four bags and a spare fuel drum in the boot.

Mum said, 'Behave yourself,' and Dad, who was not well, gave me a ten shilling note and said with a smile, 'You'll be the man on this trip.' I can't remember which was more exciting—going on this journey or having underarm hair.

Wubin was about halfway, and that was about the end of the sealed road. We filled up with petrol and headed on into the noonday sun. After about half an hour, Sonsie complained that the car was losing power, even with her foot flat to the boards. We were gradually slowing down, until finally the motor was only idling and doing about ten miles an hour and starting to overheat. We stopped in the middle of the road, because you could easily get bogged if you pulled over to the side, and there was no other traffic. Being the man, I got out and lifted the bonnet. Sonsie also had a look, but a solution didn't seem apparent. Her girlfriend and Gran stayed in the car, but with no wind coming through the windows, they both soon became wet with sweat.

Sonsie told us there was a cattle station not far up the road where her brother worked. She divided up the water and decided she and I would walk to the station to get help. We had only gone about a mile when we decided that walking in the hot desert sun was probably not a good idea, so we went back to the car.

Walking in the red dust on the side of the road, we made no noise—in fact, there was no noise anywhere. The sky was blue, the earth was red, and the scrub was dry and tormented. The old car sat quietly in the middle of the road with two people inside, and not a sound could be heard.

By the time we returned the engine had cooled down, so we decided to resume idling along at ten miles an hour for another mile or two. But when I went to close the bonnet I noticed a small spring on the engine rocker cover. This led me to the carburettor, which seemed to be where the problem was. I stretched the spring over two moveable parts, and Sonsie started the motor. This time, instead of idling, the motor raced. Sonsie quickly turned the motor off, and we came up with a strategy: if she could change gears while the engine was going flat-out, then we could more than likely get a mile or two down the road before we would be going too fast, at which time she could turn the ignition off until we slowed down, and then turn it back on again.

This worked quite well, except for a build-up of unused petrol during the ignition off-time. Whenever Sonsie turned the ignition back on again an almighty loud backfire resulted, which assured us that any wildlife or grazing cattle for miles around would be well and truly warned and not likely to be on our road.

It turned out to be lucky that we'd given up on walking to the cattle station where Sonsie's brother worked, because by the time we'd driven about ten miles this way, there was still no station. The Paynes Find cattle-watering tank seemed like a good place to stop and let the engine cool down. These water tanks were on the Shell map, and were a welcome sight out there in desert country, miles from civilisation.

Gran and I were sitting in the back. Gran was looking straight ahead, not saying a word. Sonsie told Gran that she and her girlfriend were going over to the tanks to take a swim, and that I was to stay in the car.

We wouldn't even be here if I hadn't found that spring, I said to myself. *I'm almost grown up. I've got hair under my arms and I can fix cars.* Gran didn't look like she had any sympathy for this somebody who was almost a man. I told her I was going for a walk. She said no, and told me to wait there until the girls got back. I said I had to go to the toilet, and off I went and circled around to the back of the tanks where the girls were getting undressed.

After they'd had their swim, I went back to the car. Gran was still sitting in the back seat and looking straight ahead with her ever-stern face. It was then that I realised I'd never seen her laugh. She was a very nice woman, my Gran, but jocularity wasn't one of her strong points.

Just as the girls returned, a car from the station pulled up. The driver fixed our car and then we headed to the homestead to visit Sonsie's brother. The driveway was about half a mile long, and on the way along it we stopped for a few minutes when we reached the Aboriginal stockmen's camp, which was nothing more than a few sheets of corrugated roofing tin leant up against a tree. Women, children and a bunch of scraggly dogs were sitting on the dusty red earth around a fire in the shade of the tree. A kangaroo on the fire produced a plume of blue smoke that took a toll on your nostrils as it rose above the lean-to. After the customary wave of respect, we headed off.

The main house had a compacted earth floor, hessian walls held up by local scrub timber, a tin roof and curtains instead of doors. The station manager welcomed the weary travellers, offering us cool drinks from the Coolgardie safe and a place to sit down in his well decorated main room. The walls were covered with photos of horses and jackaroos, and old-model sailing ships sat on surfaces surrounded by books and magazines. He told us it would be a while before Sonsie's brother got home from working the cattle, and offered me his bedroom for a lie-down.

Next to his bed, leaning up against the white-painted hessian, was a .303 rifle. The temptation was too great. I was twelve years old, with hair under my arms and a head full of war stories. Before I knew what I was doing, I'd moved the bolt back and forth, a bullet had entered the chamber from the magazine and the weapon was loaded. The view down the barrel was dark and foreboding. Not knowing whether anything would happen when I pulled the trigger, I pointed the heavy weapon through the window at a horse, then thought better of the idea, turned away from the window and pointed it at the hard earth floor in front of me, and pulled the trigger.

Time stood still until I was surrounded by the manager, my grandmother, Sonsie and a jackaroo, who took the rifle off me. I was standing so still my Gran asked was I hurt. When it became apparent that it was only my self-esteem that had been wounded, everyone left, taking the rifle with them. Only Gran stayed, and told me that the bullet I'd fired had ricocheted through two walls and broken a glass bottle that had housed a model sailing ship sitting on the mantelpiece in the main room. She looked me in the eye and said, 'You could have killed someone.'

I knew that my freedom for the rest of the trip would now be restricted. I was sunk like a ship; there was no excuse. Gran, with her sternest face, said that from now on I had better do exactly what I was told, or when we got back to Perth she would tell my father. With that threat hanging over me I was restricted to a few trips to the shop, and that was about it.

Chocos, my favourite lolly, were six a penny. I still had five shillings left on our last day in Mount Magnet, and five shillings' worth of Chocos filled up a large brown paper bag. But it was summer, and summers are hot in Mount Magnet, and chocolate doesn't take too kindly to hot weather, and brown paper bags can only take so much stress before they give way. When the bag split open my cousin John and I had to sit down on the side of the gravel road and eat as many as we could before they melted into the road and provided a feast for the little black ants.

The trip back to Perth was boring. No one went skinny-dipping at Paynes Find, the car didn't break down, and when we got home it seemed Gran must have thought better of telling Dad about the .303 incident.

Major changes

When I was halfway through my second year of high school, my father became seriously unwell and died. The headmaster of my school convinced my mother to keep paying the expensive school fees until the end of the year. During that time President Kennedy, whom my father respected, was shot dead by Lee Harvey Oswald, who was then shot dead by Jack Ruby, who said he hadn't done it to become a hero. Aboriginal people got to vote for the first time. Martin Luther King marched on Washington and said, 'I have a dream.' Fifteen thousand American military advisers were fighting in Vietnam.

I left school at the end of that year, laughing at silly jokes and failing every class. It wasn't that I wanted to fail, but I worried that if I was to believe all the stuff the teachers talked about, then where would that leave me as a person? Would I lose all the other things I knew, like family loyalty and how to climb a tree or catch a horse? The risk was too great. *They could ruin my life*, I thought, *by making me be one of them*. Surely there were enough people like them already.

Days after leaving school I got my first job, as a forklift driver, through my Dad's old army sergeant, who was the big boss at Wigmores, the Caterpillar tractor agent for Perth. I made my best effort at assuming a bold front as I stepped into the real world, where men talked about sex and told jokes that had finesse and timing.

When I was sixteen my mother died, and soon afterwards my grandmother passed away. Then my sister Trish joined the air force, and I bought my first car for fifty pounds. Whatever was going to happen next, I hoped it wasn't going to happen straight away. On the other hand, I also thought that maybe the more stuff that happened then, the less stuff there would be left to happen in the future.

Not long after I started at Wigmores, I realised I'd been missing the company of older people. I soon became friends with a funny and seemingly wise person named Arthur, who was older than me and who drove the store truck as his main job and was a beekeeper on the weekends. I enjoyed his company, and it wasn't long before I took an interest in bees. I started going on country trips with him, extracting honey and moving beehives around the south-west and east of Perth, depending on the seasons and honey flows. I eventually bought some hives of my own, and Arthur let me work them in with his, using his equipment.

The Fargo

Eighty-seven beehives on the back and four men in the cab was a full load, and a tight squeeze. The motor laboured and the carburettor throat hissed wide open, sucking in the air as we climbed the Bindoon hill. We changed from fourth gear down to third, and before we reached the top we were in second. Arthur, who was driving, said, 'If we slow down much more, some of us are going to have to get out and push.'

We eventually made it to the top, and the truck's biggest challenge was over for the night. The carburettor closed down to a dull hiss, then went silent as we coasted into a gravel parking area.

Arthur owned most of the beehives, but I owned twenty-three of the ones on the back of the truck. Arthur's brother-in-law Ken owned fifty-one hives at Walpole, and Arthur's dad Al didn't own any—he just came along for the company and the enjoyment of 'going bush'. He was always the last one to get into the truck, thus ensuring that he would get the window seat. I think he liked having something extra to lean against, and being the one to decide whether the window should be up or down. The cool night air didn't bother him; he would joke, 'You Australians don't know what cold is. Back in the old country this would be a heat wave.' Responding was pointless—like trying to explain to someone why a poor joke isn't funny. When the truck came to a stop

Al would sit there rigid like an old sergeant major; it didn't bother him that the rest of us had to get in and out through the driver's door.

New Norcia was our destination, and Bindoon was our halfway stopping point where we would stretch our legs, tighten the ropes and give the engine a pint of oil.

Vehicle checks done, we drove on towards the pub, discussing the pros and cons of popping in for a beer. The truck—of its own accord, it seemed—pulled up just short of the pub and parked itself under the old fig tree, which was just far enough away that the bees wouldn't be disturbed. Arthur joked that if the bees saw the lights in the pub they'd want to come in and have a drink too. Al was always the first one out on these occasions, then Ken and then Arthur; by the time I got out, Al was already at the pub door.

There were five or six men in the bar. Most said hello or nodded as we entered. We soon settled down with drinks: three beers, plus a tomato juice for me, as I was still only sixteen. The conversation was, as usual, about bees and trucks, and when that talk grew old we became quiet until someone told a joke.

When I told a joke the other men laughed, but I suspected they were just being polite. We all dressed the same, smoked cigarettes the same and were big, hardworking people: we looked, drank and talked like a team. We sat together on round wooden stools in our wax-stained overalls. Arthur ordered three more beers and asked if I was sticking with tomato juice. I said yes. We all flicked cigarette ash into the open fireplace.

In 1963, country pubs were friendly places where certain laws were regularly broken, like the ones about the drinking age and closing time. The local copper was generally respected, and kept an eye on the goings on. If a young bloke got into trouble for fighting or stealing or dangerous driving, the copper would be down at his parents' place the next day. Things would get sorted out, and more than likely that would be the end of the boy's troublemaking.

Doughy, the Bindoon publican, poured four beers and said, 'Young fellow, you can't possibly want another tomato juice.' Arthur, Ken and Al picked up their beers, but I left mine sitting on the bar. Arthur said, 'You work like a man—you can have a beer.' I thought that if I picked up that beer, maybe that would be a turning point in my life, and I wondered if I was ready. It was still sitting on the bar in front of me when the local copper came through the door. He ordered a beer and asked, 'Who owns the Fargo?'

'I do,' Arthur said.

The copper looked his way and said, 'I better not hear any complaints about bees.'

'We're just on our way,' Arthur said.

They finished their beers. I'd turned away from the bar towards the main door, when the copper said, 'It would be a terrible waste to leave that beer there, son.' I scoffed it down and headed out while the other blokes bought a couple of bottles for the road.

The carburettor hissed under the strain of the heavy load until we reached our cruising speed. The flat country was kinder to the old truck, and the talk was lighthearted. We'd had something to drink, the truck was running well, the bees were secure and calm, it was late at night, the world was dark and there was no traffic but the occasional roo bouncing across the road. Al rested against the window and snored, Ken and Arthur shared a beer and the three of us smoked cigarettes as we kept the late night awake.

New Norcia

Our apiary sites were on New Norcia Monastery property. Father Bruno had given us permission to be there, and in return wanted six gallons of honey per site every time we extracted. We had two sites on monastery property, each with around eighty hives, and during a good season we were extracting almost every three weeks. A forty-four gallon drum full of honey weighed six hundred and ninety pounds, and we would fill two or three of them in one extraction. Father Bruno kept a close eye on how much honey we were taking out, and was always there when we finished.

After a hard day's work in the sun we would head for the comfort of the pub. The New Norcia pub had two bars: one for whites and one for blacks. The black bar didn't have stools to sit on. The white bar had four stools, which meant that if there was someone else in the bar one of us would have to stand. 'The hotel', as Al would call it, stayed open late on Saturdays; as a matter of fact, I don't remember the publican ever calling last drinks, or saying it was closing time.

Saturday night was always a highlight of our trip, with a few beers and a game called skitlar, which was played on a small pool table with wooden 'men' standing in front of the holes. The table was old and did not run true: luck was essential, and Al and I were the lucky champions.

Challengers would come from everywhere—one might

be a truck driver who had broken down, another might be a farmer whose wife had gone to the city for the weekend; one time there were two painters who were staying at the hotel.

Clarence, the barman, would keep the beers coming, acting like it was a busy night with seven men in the main bar and two Aborigines in the side bar. I asked Arthur once why Aborigines weren't allowed in the main bar. 'It's the law,' he said. 'I don't agree with it, but what can you do? To me, blackfellas and whitefellas would all be the same if they were given the same opportunities.'

Short conversations sometimes said a lot, but sometimes they didn't go anywhere. Arthur made a point of not digging too deep in a conversation; in fact, most of our conversations were simple and non-judgemental, except when there were obvious heroes and villains. Billiard balls fell into holes, and truths were stretched; statements of knowledge fell to the floor and were respectfully stepped over while last drinks were drunk. The steps we took as we left the pub were deliberate, thoughtful and just a tiny bit wobbly.

Here is the news

The Sunday afternoon trip back to Perth was a quiet time. Al had an uncanny way of turning the truck radio on just as the introduction music to the national news came on.

> *Here is the news, read by James Dibble. An Australian soldier serving in Vietnam died yesterday. The Defence Department issued a statement that on Saturday June 1, 1963, Military Adviser Sergeant William Hacking died after his weapon accidently discharged when caught in vegetation. He was a non-battle casualty, and is our only fatal casualty since our deployment in that country. The Minister for Defence, Paul Hasluck, stressed that it was not a battle casualty.*

Al turned the radio off in disgust. 'The poor bloke is dead,' he said, 'so what's their point? The man was serving his country, doing a dangerous job, with a loaded rifle at the ready, when an accident happened. That's typical politician talk: they put soldiers in harm's way but then they cover their own arses when there are casualties—particularly if it's a "non-battle casualty". That poor chap died while serving his country.'

We all sat quietly, just listening to the truck's engine; several miles went by before anyone spoke.

'In that part of the world,' Al said, 'there's a vine called wait-a-while. It sticks to your clothes or your skin, and the more you fight it the more it wraps around you. I came across it during the Malay emergency in '48. It's a bastard of a thing. Young fellow, you can be thankful that you aren't going off to war.'

'Cross your fingers,' Arthur said.

Walpole

It had been a couple of months since we'd last worked the bees at Walpole, a town known for its tall trees, its sawmills and its honey. The lighter the colour of your honey, the better the price, and karri—common around the Walpole area—was the best-paying honey, at seven cents a pound. The karri only flowers every fourth year, and when it does the blossoms are so laden with nectar that some of the bees wear their wings out flying to the tops of the huge trees and then carting the nectar and pollen back to the hive. You could extract one weekend and the hives would be almost full again by the following weekend.

The only building in Walpole that was close to the main road was a corrugated iron shed. The word 'Hotel' was painted in white on a split log hanging over the entrance. It had two main rooms and a veranda along the front and down the side, which led to the toilets. One of the rooms had a skitlar table and the other was the bar, which had a fire going in it. Once inside, you could see out the back to the poorly lit 'out-the-back drinking area', which had a fire burning in a forty-four gallon drum with the top removed and some rough axe holes cut in the side for ventilation. The few people who were gathered around that fire were distinguishable only by their white teeth and white eyes; it was only when they puffed on a cigarette that you could see the outline of their faces, drinking, smoking and laughing as though their pay packets were the same size as the white men's. An Aboriginal woman holding a cloth bag sat conspicuously alone on a bench down the back.

In the main bar, men stood two deep, some with their open yellow pay packets in their hand or in their shirt pocket; others who were lucky enough to have found a stool left their pay packets safely on the bar, even when they went to the toilet.

As I headed to the toilets, I passed a big bald-headed bloke, who I later found out was the mill foreman, with his arm around an Aborigine's shoulder. This is a friendly town, I thought. And it turned out you couldn't even go to the dunny without hearing a story.

'Did you hear what happened today?' a bloke at the washbasin said.

The man at the urinal answered, 'What was that?'

'Jacky saved the foreman's son from certain death. They were out chainsawing a new logging path when it happened. He almost cut his leg off, and if it hadn't been for Jacky covering the wound with honey and tightly wrapping his shirt around it, he would have died with all the loss of blood. Aborigines, mate, I tell you, are the smartest people on earth.'

Back inside, Jacky was the only Aborigine in the main bar, and even with a few beers under his belt he still didn't look comfortable. His hands looked swollen from beestings, and he kept looking back over his shoulders and moving his feet about. Finally he said to his boss, 'My real name is Jarrah.'

'Jarrah it is, then,' said the foreman. 'That's a fine name, and I'll tell you something else, too: next Friday night you come straight into the main bar, and if there's a seat available you sit in it and put your pay envelope on the bar, like everyone else, and if anyone says anything, you send them over to see me.'

Jarrah shook hands with his boss and walked out through the front door. His wife stood up and, with her cloth bag under her arm, followed behind her husband as they walked back to their camp.

We left the Walpole pub in fine spirits and drove slowly into the bush. The headlights barely penetrated the misty night; the tree canopy was thick, and moonlight couldn't help.

First we followed a muddy track to the end of the sawmill property, then with the truck headlights on high beam we made our own track through the bush where some large trees had recently been cut down. When we recognised the base of a stand of trees by their huge girths, we knew we were close.

We made a turn down a gentle slope and Arthur turned off the motor. The only noise to be heard was the bees flapping their wings to maintain the hive temperature; we could smell the bees and the honey. A low mist covered the apiary site, and sitting on what looked like a cloud were the top boxes of our hives.

I was sleeping in the firebreak between the truck and a fence, in my dad's khaki canvas pink-wool-lined World War II sleeping bag. My dad had slept in that bag in El Alamein, Egypt, Tobruk, Libya, Kokoda and Borneo, where conditions were so harsh that I bet he kept his .303 rifle inside his bag when he went to sleep. Though the night was cold and damp, my dad's sleeping bag was more than capable of looking after me; even the rain and animal noises didn't bother me.

Morning came and the sun trickled into our apiary. Birds made their noises, white-tailed rabbits scampered through the fence and the thumping of leaves warned that the big grey kangaroos were on the move. For the first time I saw ice hanging from a fence like a stalactite. A big grey casually jumping over the fence from the other side must have got a shock when he looked down and saw me, because as I looked up his tail slammed down onto the top wire and the ice fell to the ground. I was warm and unafraid in my dad's army sleeping bag. I was almost completely brave.

The tall skinny grass was bent over with the weight of the morning frost. Al was getting a fire going to make tea before we started loading the bees. It was too early for talking. I got up and stood by the fire; staring at it prepared my empty head for the heavy tasks ahead.

We loaded the bees onto the truck and headed north. After driving for about five or six hours the itch and swelling of the beestings had gone, and with our tired conversation at a lull, cheerful thoughts of cold beer were once again firmly in our minds—among one or two other thoughts, like, were the bees still on the back?, and, gee, I'm thirsty.

Al and the cop story

We were too late to find a pub still legally open, but as luck would have it we found a pub back door that was known to be friendly to travellers. After a couple of cold beers we got back into the truck and stories of past adventures began to ricochet around the truck once more as if being told for the first time.

Al, who had a slight memory problem, told his favourite story with the same excitement as when he'd first told it a year ago. I think he must have forgotten that I was on that trip too, because he looked at me until he was sure he had my attention before he began.

'Mundaring Shire,' he said, 'had the strictest, meanest copper in WA, but we beat him—twice.' Al's face would light up when he told this story, just the same as it did when he told a war story. 'Once was when he was on his motorbike. He pulled us up for speeding, and when he saw our load of bees he took two steps back and said, "Get the hell out of here."

'The other time was when we were heading for the whitegum honey in York. The copper was in his new shiny blue police car. Ken didn't come on that trip, so Arthur had invited his friend, the Assistant Commissioner of Police, who'd been pestering us to come on one of our weekend trips. I told the Commish, "No disrespect intended, but you will never see a beekeeper wearing blue. Bees hate blue, and that's a fact." Anyway, we were driving through Mundaring when

Wiggsy, the cop, pulled us over and demanded to know what was in the drums. "They're empty," Arthur said. The copper said, "Hey, smart arse, I think you're carting petrol. You get up on the back and open the bungs." "The drums are empty, but the hives are full of bees," Arthur told him, "and if you keep us here with your flashing blue lights, you're going to have a police car full of bees." Wiggsy said, "Get out of the truck," and the Assistant Commissioner of Police said, "Officer, what is your police badge number?" Wiggsy said, "And just who the hell are you?" "I am the Assistant Commissioner of Police, WA," the Commish replied. "Now what is your badge number?"'

Travelling from childhood to semi-adulthood was a slow process. I was fortunate to be in the company of two good, patient men who showed respect and tolerance towards me, and of Al, the old soldier.

Mr. Arthur E. George,

Dampier Mining,

KOOLAN ISLAND, W. A., 6733.

Registration No. 5019765

During

CALL-UP

You are hereby called
Military Forces of the Commonwealth

You are required to pr

This notice should be
Certificate of Registration

Enclosed are travel warr
your journey from Koolan Island to Der
cintly been advised to Perth. Departu
will depart Koolan Island at 7.30 a.m.
will travel to you Perth by MMA
1968. At Perth, on 1st Oct, you will board
12.45 p.m. on 1st October, 1968. On t
the warrants you will be supplied with

National Service call-up

Before the army took me away, I lived and worked up north as a deckhand on an old army landing barge for BHP. Life was simple and easy. Conversation didn't drift much past boats or fishing. Time passed slowly, as anything significant rarely happened.

Each morning I'd secure the barge for travel and make a cup of tea. The skipper preferred beer, even first thing in the morning. On weekdays before he left camp, he'd wrap four cold longneck stubbies in newspaper, then wrap a towel around them and tuck them neatly into his canvas bag to keep them cold during the hot dusty trip on the back of the truck to the wharf. By the time we got out to the barge they'd still be cool, and each time he finished a bottle he'd fill it from the water bag and drop it over the far side of the barge so the people on the wharf couldn't see. Then he'd say, 'There goes another dead marine,' or, with his Irish accent, 'I think we'll have to give this one the flotation test.'

As you can see, there wasn't a lot to talk about.

On Saturdays he'd bring six in his canvas bag. It was a very ordinary bag, but it had character. Some of the wharfies took identical canvas bags to work. Some carried fishing gear so they could fish in their lunch break. Curly, the cook—who wasn't really a cook but was in charge of the crib room—carried very sharp knives wrapped in a towel. I never understood why he didn't just leave his knives in the crib room, and why the other guys didn't just leave their fishing gear in their lockers in the crib room.

Everyone seemed to recognise everyone else's canvas bag. If a bag was left on the transport truck or on the barge, everyone would know whose bag it was and would pay it due respect. The skipper's bag bulged a bit more than the others.

Sometimes when we were working at sea, unloading a state ship at night, he would send me up the rope ladder with his bag to ask the bursar of the ship to sell me some beer. In fact, he preferred beer so much that sometimes the whole job was left to me, and still it was easy—nothing physical or mental—just driving a barge around, picking up wharf labourers, unloading state ships at sea; food and beer supplies, mostly.

The BHP workers on Koolan and Cockatoo islands were non-union, unlike those on the state ships, so they often protested against us by not tying up at our wharf and making us unload at sea. When the sea was rough it was something to talk about, and added character to our job description. Still, life was a breeze. After work there was fishing and swimming and, on Saturdays, movies or the pub.

Then one day I got a letter from my sister, saying she'd called up the National Service mob to find out if I was going to be called up. For some unknown reason they'd said I was already in the army, and thanks for the call. She'd said, 'No, he's not, he's working up north.'

A few days later I got a telegram delivered personally by our not-very-tall postman, normally a bright and cheerful person, but on this occasion he wasn't smiling. A few of his friends were with him. I seemed to be the focus of their attention. I thought somebody must have died and the concerned postman's friends had come down to the wharf as a show of support.

I looked at the sealed telegram, and then back to the frowning postman with his entourage. I suspected they all knew what was in the telegram. Life was simple, and I started to wish that he hadn't given me this envelope. But I opened it anyway, and started to read.

Tension hit me between the eyes, just like the time I'd walked into the hook on the wharf crane. The not-very-tall postman and his friends suggested we go to the pub.

I looked down, trying to fathom what was happening. Everybody and everything I could see suddenly had new meanings, like they were in the past tense. The trip on the back of the truck to the pub was uneventful; my grip on the handrail was tight, for the feeling for where I was was diminishing.

We read the telegram many times. It was notification from the Department of Labour and National Service that I was to be conscripted into the Australian Army. Travel orders had been dispatched, and I should pack my bags with the intention of not returning to Yampi Sound, as the medical and entrance tests should be straightforward.

The beers were flowing; I felt lightheaded. The only thing I was sure about was that somebody else was going to be in control of my life for the next two years. It almost took my breath away.

Naive traveller

On the plane heading down to Perth I met another bloke who had also been conscripted. We talked about where we'd worked and our different jobs and the amount of money we'd made.

He seemed to know a lot about how much people got paid, like that our army pay would start off at $57.00 a fortnight and wouldn't get much better.

'I was paying more than that in tax every week,' I said.

'Me too,' he said, adding, 'Adam's the name.'

'Ted,' I said, and stuck my hand up, showing two fingers to the air hostess. 'Two more Swan lagers,' I called. 'I'm as dry as a dead dingo's donger.'

Up north during the early days of iron ore mining and railway construction, huge amounts of money were paid to draw workers to sites with virtually no civilised amenities. I'd enjoyed the high wages and never given much thought to the amount of tax we paid. But some of the blokes—especially the foreigners from England and Scotland—were always complaining that we were taxed too high and got nothing in return.

Adam reckoned these taxes paid for the blokes down in Perth to get a completely free education at the university, and furthermore, he said, some of these blokes only went to university to get out of being called up into the army to do their National Service.

I could see Adam was a deep thinker. Quite a few times on that trip south I had to say, 'Empties only,' or, 'It's your shout, mate.'

'You know,' he said at one point, 'in forty years' time we could get a service pension or, if we get injured, a disability pension. Those blokes that joined the university just to get out of being called up, I hope they remember us in forty years' time when they have a high-paying job, and don't complain that their taxes are paying for our pensions. I hope they'll understand who we are.'

Three ranks

Several hundred twenty-year-old boys assembled on the lawns of the Karrakatta army base. We were processed, fed and numbered, then put into small groups of consecutive numbers.

A bunch of people in army clothes with loud voices advised us that we were now in the army and subject to its rules and discipline. Our first order was to form three ranks on the quadrangle—a simple task, once you knew what three ranks were and what a quadrangle was. Fortunately we had these people dressed in green politely advising us, adding with just a hint of sarcasm in their voices that they might not always be this polite, especially if you were talking in the ranks or if you had long hair or a beard.

Sitting on the grass, wondering what would happen next, a rumour spread that we were heading for the airport where six commercial aircraft were waiting to fly us to Victoria.

We took off around midnight from Perth Airport, and arrived at Mangalore airport in Victoria on a cold morning before the sun had come up. We were then loaded into the backs of army trucks and taken to Puckapunyal, where the corporals and sergeants were not so polite.

'Line up on the road in columns of three!' the corporal yelled. 'No talking—move it! When I say move it, I mean move it—now! Or are you all a bit slow over there in the West?'

Early-morning wake-ups were something we soon got used to, with a corporal banging a big stick on a rubbish-bin lid and yelling, 'Three ranks on the quadrangle—now—move, move, move. Stand to attention, fists clenched, thumbs pointing down, keep those fingers still or I'll break them off and stick the wet end up your nose.'

For three months we marched around that square, did fitness and weapons training and learned about army discipline and what was expected of us. We were given reasons to be proud that we were in the Australian Army. Loyalty was essential; without it, we were told, we were a dead dog's breakfast.

The following three months for me were spent completing engineer core training in Casula in New South Wales. Friendships developed, and we were starting to get an idea of what was expected of us. The novelty of building something and then blowing it up maintained our boyish interest, but delousing mines and booby traps had a more serious tone.

Saturday nights, if we weren't on duty, I headed with my new mates Buj (Joe Bujnowski) and Tony Mac to Kings Cross. The Whisky à Go Go club catered to American GIs with lots of money to spend on their seven days' R&R leave from Vietnam. There were dancing girls, flashing lights and loud music. The bar was packed full with these strange-talking men, yelling to be heard. Instant friendships were being made, just because they came from the same state or liked the same baseball team. There were hundreds of them in twos and threes, yet they were all joined together by something I was only just beginning to understand.

The last part of our indoctrination was three weeks' jungle training in Canungra in Queensland. Once that was completed we were ready to go to war, and subject to active service military law. We were told of the severe consequences if we fucked up. For instance, if we went absent without leave we could be charged with desertion in front of the enemy, and could be shot. Fitness and discipline were the order of the day; boyish behaviour and simple humour were soon put in their place and were replaced by army humour, where the bottom line was about survival, mateship and staying alive.

We learned jungle survival skills, more weapons training and what we could expect from the enemy, and we did one hell of a lot of running around.

That was our final preparation for Vietnam. All ground forces had to do it. Some were more ready than others. Buj, Tony and I had bigger builds than most, and at twenty years of age fitness was not a problem, but mentally we were still boys: we thought we were bulletproof.

Good morning, Vietnam

Getting off a plane in a strange place—a place at war—was so serious that a joke did not even come to mind. The noise of gunships, of medevac choppers with the Red Cross on their sides and underneath, of the jet fighters and the bombers, and the thought of all the young men who had died and the responsibility we had towards them and their families, was overwhelming.

Do the right thing. This is now. This is real. If we're good and we do as we're told, history will report on us well, overlooking the other dimensions of death and injury.

Saigon was thirty-four miles from the China Sea. Its river was one of the delta streams that fed the Mekong: this information seemed important at the time. We were sitting on our sausage bags at the end of a runway, jet-fuel smells and tropical heat presenting a new atmosphere. The runway and the sky were busy: aircraft were taking off or landing every twenty seconds. It was said to be the busiest airport in the world.

Waiting there for a Hercules to take us on the final trip to our base camp seemed normal. Information was passed on sparingly, but it didn't matter; we were under orders now, and had learnt to do what we were told and to trust the person who gave the order. There was a serious intensity in our boyish faces.

The next time we heard a death count, we might know that person as a friend. I couldn't talk without intense concentration. A sign of respect for the dead, I suppose—and maybe a sign that, as a result of our loyalty training in particular, death would not be the most important thing, and that where we were was such a serious place that all we could rely on was the narrow focus of the last seven months. I knew we would always be loyal to those we could no longer drink with, and who we would see and hear in our hearts forever.

Arriving at Nui Dat, where our base camp would be, I was assigned to a four-man hut. It was a tent with sandbags around it and a plaque on the centre pole saying 'Death before dishonour'. I wondered if I was worthy of dying in such company, or whether these people were just a little over the top.

A few weeks later we built a hut with a concrete floor, a tin roof and a light, which we had to turn off at night, naturally; no sense in asking for trouble. There was another shed at the other end of our camp called the boozer. The beer was very cheap, and it helped one and all in many ways.

Bobby's white dress

Bobby was the odd man out. He didn't drink or smoke or even spit, so his search for friendship and common bonding was difficult. His spare time was spent writing to his wife or playing card games like patience. He taught me how to play euchre and 500, and he often told little stories about his life. Not a complicated man, and desperate to hang onto his rural Queensland roots, he was a bit religious (as needed), decent, God-fearing (as needed), a rightwing political Joh Bjelke-Petersen supporter and not a hard person to understand—except for the story of the white dress.

In telling us that his wife had worn a white dress to their wedding, he was confirming his standards—and revealing his moral insecurities. There was no one else around to back him up: unfortunately, he was all alone, and he couldn't change who he was. It was as though he was afraid of what might happen. Now was not the time for change, so I went along with the white dress story.

'Euchre?' Bobby said to me one day.

'Yep,' I said. 'The boozer's not open yet.'

'I don't drink,' he said. 'Out on the farm in Queensland, after work we drink lemonade or tea, and play cards.'

'In Perth we work during the day and drink beer at night,' I replied.

He showed me a picture of his wife.

'She wore a white dress when we were married,' he said. 'Do you know what that means?'

'Nah.'

'Well, it means she was a virgin.' Then he whispered, 'So was I.'

I whispered back, 'Are you glad about that?'

'Yeah,' he replied. 'We think that's really important.'

Bobby was anxious for common ground—*his* common ground. It was probably best that he didn't try to change. His face was suntanned, thin and clean. A long nose pointed in the direction of least resistance. The occasional smirk indicated that he was a man.

Wouldn't it be grand if life were that simple? At times I felt anger that he treated life with such little respect.

We often played cards and we both cocked our weapons as we left camp. At least we had that in common. We were comrades to some degree.

Fox hole

It was dark. A big-feeling spider crawled over my hand. Guns and rifles were sounding, the crackling of a VC rocket sounded overhead. It landed on the mess. One man died.

The spider didn't bite. The earth felt safe on my arms and neck. Something crawled over my arm. I wasn't scared. I felt safe with nature and I longed for that warm empty feeling in my head, far away from the noise of guns, rifles and rockets.

Underpants Mervin

There were five other guys I lived with, starting with the least notable:

Jock: the less said the better.

Euchre Bobby.

Bob, also known as Ferret.

Lorrie.

Billy: salt of the earth.

And Underpants Mervin.

Jock had the personality of a down-on-his-luck car salesman.

Euchre Bobby, with his white dress, you know about.

Ferret was notable back in Australia for opening up an E-type Jag with an old-fashioned can opener, gaining entry, coasting down the hill from the Whisky à Go Go in Kings Cross and crashing. 'In-country', he went on a liquid diet. He had troubles and wasn't talking. I think it would be fair to say that he did not want to be there.

Lorrie was just married, conscripted and dragged away. Cool, kind and hip, he was gradually eaten up with hatred for where he was and despair for where he wanted to be. As the days grew longer, the sadder he got with the growing knowledge that his life would never be the same.

Billy was the salt of the earth. Some people are born nice and stay nice. If cloning humans goes ahead, I hope they get Billy's DNA.

Underpants Mervin did things his own way.

When I arrived in-country, a few things were pointed out to me. Sleep here, eat there, toilet there, supplies and weapons there. Mark your jungle greens with a texta and leave them there for the local laundry company.

'What about underpants?'

'No one in this country wears them.'

It felt like the first day of school all over again, but not a gum tree in sight.

For the next twelve months it was green socks, green pants, green shirts and GP boots. Nothing else existed. Any personal items, like underpants, were locked away in your steel trunk—except for Mervin's. A few days after Mervin's arrival, there, hanging on a wire, fluttering in the sun—white, no less—were Mervin's underpants.

Mervin used to get migraines at night. He got quite delirious; it was like he was having a nightmare, but he couldn't wake up. He was talking and moaning. It lasted for hours sometimes. With such a problem, I wondered how he'd got into the army. He was pretty well confined to camp. No sleepovers with the grunts, no patrols, no track work, no land clearing. While the rest of us were out doing exciting things like blowing up stuff or building a windmill in a village, Mervin was back in camp.

It's funny how things seem to fit. He probably needed that time in camp to wash his underpants.

The other Bob

There was a third Bob—he sometimes just appeared when some of us were a bit confused about what was happening. 'It's okay,' he would say. He was complicated and completely in control of the personal situation. He was smart and reserved and a skilful manipulator of conversation. Even the officers avoided him. They couldn't keep up with his fast mind and confident demeanour. I once saw him install a light at the head of an officer's bed with the switch on the top so that when the officer turned the light off at night he would probably burn his hand on the hot bulb. Bob enjoyed tinkering on the edge, putting others off balance and then returning them to their foundations when they needed it most.

'It's the little things that count as you go through life,' he told me. 'Whenever there are confrontations, particularly with officers, tell them Bob said it was okay. With the higher-ranking officers this will be met with instant approval. With the younger lieuies, look them straight in the eye; don't wave the red flag, but let them retreat with dignity.' I felt comfortable with this Bob.

Before I'd started my National Service I'd done some work as a tradesman's assistant. The pay was good. The satisfaction was nil. A tradesman was respected; a TA wasn't. If you offered conversation about the job you were looked at with disdain, and if you said anything that might have been useful you were looked at with suspicion. Your human spirit was shot down with the words 'fucking TAs'.

We were mining iron ore at Koolyanobbing, the local Aboriginal name for 'place of large hard rocks'. One night I asked the mechanic a question. He looked at me, all sincere, and replied, 'Trade secret. I'm not giving away the secrets. I'm a tradesman. Now go and make the tea.'

I can't remember his name. He was very white, a puffy face, about thirty-five years old, slightly overweight, and had a nervous wife with a lazy tongue.

There was no fresh milk that night, so mixing the powdered milk with cold water was the trick. The mechanic, what's-his-name, asked how I made the tea without lumps in the milk. 'Trade secret,' I said, and refused to tell him the cold-water trick.

Anyway, over there, in the army, we all worked together. Information was shared. Everybody had some skills—mental or physical or trained tradesman. I think we were all glad to work together, even the fucking officers. This might help to explain the expression 'You had to be there'.

Bob knew tons and gave it away by the bucketful, and yet you knew he kept a tantalising amount in reserve.

What was he protecting? Memories, ambition, or the intense sadness that nothing would ever be the same? He did have a lot to give, so what was he protecting? Was it Sir Bob, twelve-inch Bob, or the Bob that got away?

One thing was for sure: he was in control of his personality. Perhaps it was at breaking point. And his boots were just clean enough not to arouse suspicion.

I sit here, we sat there

Two of us were on lookout duty while our earthmoving crew was digging a trench to be used as a slipway for fishing boats. The major in charge of our squadron was eager to help the local people in an effort to gain their support in the fight against the communist North Vietnamese enemy.

We sat there on a sandy hilltop in the open, with nothing to hide behind; rifles and a couple of two-way radios were our only comforts. The enemy was not far away, so there was good reason for a bit of apprehension.

We were overlooking a small fishing village; its navigation leads embraced the South China Sea. The water was blue, as was the narrow channel to the fishing village about a half a mile away. To the sides of the channel was mangrove swamp, flat and muddy. At low tide you could see pockets of deep water surrounded by mud, consistent with the pattern B52 bombers leave. The bombers hadn't made those holes in the ground—they didn't drop bombs where we were—but when you're on foreign land in the middle of a war, something like those holes in the ground is important to claim: 'Our side made those holes.' 'We did that.' 'The other side hasn't made as many holes in the ground as we have.'

The fishing boats came in with their catch of mud crabs, shellfish and an assortment of small fish. The black boats with diesel engines were long and heavy, made with thick teak planks, and needed the deepest part of the mangrove channel to stay afloat.

The tide ran over silky brown mud without any visible signs of life other than a group of locals rummaging around in the mud, who were of little concern to us as long as they were doing innocent things. They were about three hundred yards away. Two adults were digging and five or six kids were sifting through the upturned mud.

'You'd have to be a good shot from here,' I said, with carefree bravado. The truth was, I was talking up courage and trying to keep calm. It was partly to let my partner know that we were in charge of this hill and that we would decide what went on around here.

We were a close-knit outfit—there was no them and us—we were all in the army and that was it. Anyone who wasn't was the enemy. Civilians, like those villagers, were not trusted, and therefore not respected. There was only our army. Although we supported other armies—the ARVN, the Kiwis, the Yanks, Thailand, Korea and others—we really only relied on our army.

'A good shot? You mean that forty-four gallon drum down there near that family of shellfish gatherers?' my mate said.

'That's right, near those little people.'

'How will we know if we hit it?' he said.

'If it's an old petrol drum, with the cap sealed, it will probably explode,' I replied.

We were so confident we wouldn't hit that family. We fired away. We were so confident. We were not out of control. We were professionals having a shoot. The little people down below scattered like ants into the last remaining vegetation. I thought they would be cooler in those bushes. Anyway, they were safer where they were than we were where we were.

Our actions might not seem to be those of normal people. All I can say is that we weren't in a normal situation. Life and death were confronted with live ammunition.

Two bottles of beer

The main man in the fishing village came up our hill and said, 'My house: bomb, booby trap. You come see, now.'

His house was a four-poster with straw on top. What a craftsman: not a nail in sight, just incredible woodwork. An old table and two chairs sat on a dirt floor, a bed and some more straw lay at the end of the hut. If he hadn't been so pushy, I would probably have felt sorry that some little bugger had planted a grenade outside his front door.

The possibility of it being booby trapped was real.

'Booby trap,' the fisherman said, nodding.

'We get clearance for big bang,' I said. 'You bring beer and ice to top of hill.'

Back on the hill we dug a hole about two feet deep and two feet square. We lined it with a rainproof poncho. When the villager returned we put in the ice and the two bottles of beer.

'Two beers not enough,' we told him. 'You are rich man, with many houses and fishing boats and slipway, and this is dangerous job.'

We had already radioed in for a clearance to blow the grenade up, and the guy knew it.

'You get ready,' he told us. 'Do job now. Like your boss say, you must improve relations.'

'Okay.' Back down the hill we went to the four-poster hut.

To one side of the entrance, half-buried in mud, was an M26 grenade, now partly exposed by last night's tropical rain. Sometimes the enemy would create a nuisance like that just to let everybody know they were around. If they really wanted to make a stronger point they would booby trap the grenade with an anti-lifting device.

What with the tension and being short-changed on the beer by that pushy little fellow, I decided to increase the charge from half a pound to two pounds of plastic explosive—that should sort a few things out.

Then we found a place to take cover from the explosion. The most obvious places might also be booby trapped; they were smart little buggers.

Well, after the big bang, we were all a little sorry: him, whose roof was now scattered with the wind all over the South China Sea, and us, with no beer and a wet poncho.

On lookout

The next day was Melbourne Cup Day. I was still on top of the same hill, and I wondered if Ho Chi Minh knew about the Melbourne Cup. We were all wondering about him, for it had been reported on American forces radio that Uncle Ho had recently died, but nobody here believed it, especially the locals.

Later on that day, one of the APC drivers came up the hill and asked if I would transmit the Cup on their frequency. I picked up the ABC broadcast to South-East Asia and transmitted the 1969 Melbourne Cup on the APC work channel.

Our headquarters, Alpha 8, was not impressed. 'This is a works network,' some fucking officer said. So I confirmed: 'Rain Lover has won the Cup.'

I spotted our major driving past with a red flag on his jeep. The red flag was a signal to us that he was aware that he was travelling on an enemy-controlled road, so do not stop him.

He was a nice bloke, the major. Really, they were all good blokes. We sometimes lightheartedly called them 'fucking officers', just because, after all, they were in charge of what was going on. It seemed only fair.

No one else said a thing about the transmission except a couple of blokes from the armoured personnel carriers, who radioed back, 'Good on ya,' and, 'Thanks, mate.' Those blokes had the most dangerous job of all.

The next day we were in another fishing village assembling a Southern Cross windmill. Tension was high, as the ground was littered with bits of old metal, tin cans and shrapnel, which made it almost impossible to use the mine detector. The mayor told us there was an unmarked old French minefield right next to the windmill site, so be careful.

It seemed a bit odd installing the windmill because they already had a fast-running freshwater creek, but you do as you're told and with a bit of luck you might get some time off to visit the local bar.

The village wasn't far from the hilltop where we were on lookout. It was a pretty village. A light haze of smoke from cooking pots covered the thatched roofs, and the smell of spicy food reminded us that we were far from home. Late in the day, with an hour or so before we were to head back to camp, my mate and I found the bar.

We had the local beer, called Thirty-three, poured warm out of the bottle into a scratched plastic glass, like a milkshake glass, and then topped up with slightly off-colour chipped block of ice with a few black wooden splinters in it.

We sat on a grey wooden bench wearing green clothes and black boots. The building had a warm friendly feel about it, but the few other people who were there soon finished their drinks and left through the open doorway. The mama-san delivered our next drinks without a smile, and quickly returned to behind the bar.

We sat there, and I wondered if I would ever see a Melbourne Cup, or go to a high-school reunion back at my old private boys' grammar school in Perth and get to ask my old classmates, 'How come you fuckers didn't get called up and go to Vietnam?'

We held plastic beakers in one hand and rifles in the other.

The grass window shutters were propped up with sticks and the peaceful sound of the creek entered the bar. It was a pity we couldn't let go of our rifles.

A forty-ounce bottle of whisky

Being a lateral thinker has its drawbacks, because there is no final solution. Of course, military discipline was a problem, and even before that, work, school, even kindergarten.

Lateral thinkers don't have it that easy, so it's just as well we can think sideways and not get bogged down with so-called normal thoughts.

I knew it was a serious breach of army discipline to smuggle a bottle of whisky back to camp at Nui Dat, so I didn't think about it. Even though the warm buzz in my face warned me, at the same time it excused me. The buzz was strong at times, producing exhilarating feelings and contempt for conformity.

I had about two hours to wait for a convoy to assemble that would transport men and equipment from Vung Tau to Nui Dat. I never did like waiting.

About half a mile down the road was the US air base, and it had a store called the 'PX'. I had heard some American solders say it was 'just like downtown'. You could buy anything there: cameras, radios, whisky, and reel-to-reel tape recorders.

PX stood for postal exchange, and its purpose was to allow US servicemen to send home some of their pay, and to buy duty-free goods cheaply before their tour of duty finished and they returned to their so-called world.

I imagined that when I was due to go home I would do the same thing, but I wondered about the importance of taking duty-free things home from a war. Was it a distraction, a reward, or perhaps just a tradition—like when you go away on holidays and return with presents? Someone would say, 'How was it over there?' And you would say, 'Look what I've got in this box,' and you wouldn't feel bad, because you'd have a new reel-to-reel tape recorder that filled up a lot of space.

It was a hot gravel road. To the sides was a small wire fence with periodic signs saying 'Keep Out—Landmines' and 'Defoliant Chemicals—Keep Out'.

On my belt I had two water bottles and six magazines— the one on my rifle made seven. I walked fast. It was an eerie place. The bushes on both sides were dead: some lay dead on the ground, while others stood in a non-conforming way, but dead just the same.

On the silent horizon was the air base. I was too far away to hear the planes and helicopters that were dancing around like flies. It was quiet where I was, no traffic. I looked around front and back and had second thoughts about where I was; I wondered if I had made a mistake in coming down this road. Ah, what were you going to do when you've got the buzz? I believed no harm was going to come to me, and anyway, the journey was there for the taking.

It was a hot hazy day, with sand blowing around the lifeless bush, and I was halfway between nowhere and the PX. The buzz in my cheeks was the only support I had.

A small figure appeared, coming from the air base. With the sun behind him, he looked like he was dressed in black. I drew on that warm buzz in my cheeks. I held my weapon close, my grip tightening as the figure approached. Weapon ready and safety catch off. The warmth from my cheeks was now on my ears, and I really hoped I wouldn't have to make a decision.

The black figure without a visible weapon kept coming like a shadow. As we got closer, now a hundred yards away, the shadow grew lighter.

I wished he was carrying a weapon, so I could tell which side he was on. I could see he was not wearing black or grey, but khaki. He was in his travel uniform. There was something shining on his collar. No one in a war zone wears shiny things. Maybe they do in a John Wayne movie, but not here.

We were almost at talking distance when I recognised that he was a second lieutenant in the US Army, unarmed, in an ironed class-A travel uniform and wearing his rank on his collar. It must have been his first day in-country; he must have just landed and been taking a stroll.

We had been warned that some of the American soldiers did not have a lot of training; hardly enough time even to forget their civilian life before they were in a combat zone. This stranger was not in my army, and he was an officer—we could not have been further apart. As we passed we didn't speak; I just winked and he gestured with half a smile.

The PX was packed with all the latest electrical stuff—lots of reel-to-reel tape recorders, the new single-reflex cameras, and large bottles of whisky.

I opted for the forty-ounce bottle of Johnny Walker Red Label. How I managed to get it back to camp was a miracle, it really was a miracle, and this happened in a place where there were no miracles no matter how much a soldier begged for one.

A paper bag concealed my joy. There was nowhere to hide it on my belt and my backpack was in camp, so I pretended it wasn't out of place, even when I got back to the convoy that was ready to move out. Bouncing in the back of a jeep on the way to Nui Dat my eyes were a little warm with the buzz, but no one asked me what was in the bag.

Back in camp I walked to my hutch alone, like I was carrying a Mother's Day present.

In the hot sober evening, hiding the whisky in my pack, I realised how much trouble I would be in if I got caught. Sleep was the only thing that rescued me from the worry.

No worries

The next morning, after a good breakfast, two mates and I were detailed to search for mines and booby traps on a construction site in Baria. Our mob was building an extra room for the hospital that was run by the Spanish nuns, the Sisters of Mercy. I was relaxed; we had been on this detail several times and not much had happened. Loading up the aluminium suitcases that held the mine detectors and checking that they were in good working order, I noticed that there was just enough room in my case for a mine detector and a forty-ounce bottle of whisky—so in she went.

We were joined on the truck by two carpenters, a bricklayer, a concrete man, a truck driver and, next to him, our new sergeant. On the back of the truck were two bench seats running down the middle, so we all faced outwards, in case we were attacked.

It's not a very long drive to Baria, and as we left the camp checkpoint I wondered briefly what I was going to do with the whisky. I pulled it out of the aluminium case, and my two mates on my side of the truck frowned for a second.

The guys on the other side of the truck were looking in the opposite direction; the sergeant was up front. We were travelling reasonably fast, and the three of us realised we had privacy.

I opened the bottle, and the wind took the cap away. I took a swallow and handed it to Ferret; he took a gulp or two and passed it on. When it came back to me I took another swig, then Ferret took another drink or two, and this went on until we reached Baria, where I threw the empty bottle into a rice paddy.

While we were unloading our equipment, Ferret fell backwards off the truck and landed on a sand pile, laughing uncontrollably. This attracted some of the local kids, who joined in the laughing.

'What's the matter with him?' the sergeant asked.

'Just a joke,' I said. But Ferret kept on laughing, and the sergeant suspected he was still drunk from yesterday's leave.

'Call Alpha 8,' he said to the truck driver. 'We need a pick-up; he's a danger to himself and everyone around him.'

Ferret tried to stand up.

'We'll look after him, Sergeant,' I said, 'and do his share of the work. He'll be in a pile of shit if you send him back.'

'Yeah, don't send him back,' a couple of the other blokes chipped in.

It was the sergeant's first day on the job, and he took more notice of us than he normally might have. While Ferret slept under a tree, I swept a mine detector over the pile of building sand that the kids were playing on. The kids were friendly and helpful while we were looking for mines. I named one of them, who was slightly overweight, 'Little Buddha'. He was a handy person to know.

'How come you hang around here in the mornings?' I asked him.

'There's morning school and afternoon school,' he replied. 'Morning school is 7 am to noon. I go to school between noon and 5 pm.' His English was quite good. 'When you see us kids playing around here, don't worry, no VC. When you don't see us, watch out, VC,' he said.

'I heard on the American forces radio that Ho Chi Minh died,' I said.

'Never happen, baby,' he said. 'Uncle Ho never die.'

A few minutes later I was quickly sobered up by the scream of my mine detector, which almost sent me into orbit. Little Buddha stepped back a little, his eyes focused on me for a few seconds, then he shook his head. 'Never happen, baby.'

Careful prodding revealed a shovel that someone had left in the sand pile.

I stood up with warm cheeks and a dry mouth. The morning sun was on the back of my neck and I wondered about life and what time it was in Maida Vale.

When you think you might be in the hands of someone who likes you but who has been dead for a long time, you wonder about God, faith and luck.

ARVN training camp

A resupply chopper dropped me off on the outskirts of Dat Do, where I met up with a mate I'd gone through core training with. Tony was the number one in a two-man mini-team assigned to land clearing in the Long Hai hills. He told me his number two had been ordered back to Nui Dat, and that I would be his temporary replacement, working with Tony on an APC.

We loaded the supplies into the APC and headed off to a nearby ARVN training camp that would be our base. Tempting fate, we briefly stopped in town to buy a crushed ice and pineapple drink from a street vendor. Keeping in touch with doing normal, non-military things eased the tension. Tony talked about his family and showed me a picture that he kept in his wallet of his wife and new daughter.

The mini-team's job was to look for signs of mines. Often this could be just a broken stick in the ground, three small rocks stacked on top of each other, a machete mark in a tree or anything that was slightly unnatural: this would warn the other VC fighters of a mine. Our mission was to support the bulldozer operators who were clearing the vegetation around where the VC was hiding.

The bulldozer drivers, the APC crew, Tony and I made camp at one end of the training camp; the local recruits were doing a night practice shoot at their rifle range at the other end. Tony, myself and the two blokes from the APC decided to visit the ARVN officers mess for a beer.

The barman and one officer were both leaning on the bar, drinking out of rice wine cups. They were the only people in the mess, which was a large corrugated tin building full of empty tables and chairs. We decided to sit a respectful distance from those two men.

A young ARVN recruit snuck in through a side entrance and quietly pulled up a chair next to us. He was full of happiness and wanted to talk to us 'tourists' so badly that he ignored the consequences of what might happen to him.

'Didi mau!' (a rude way of saying 'leave') a voice cried out. The recruit turned red, and seconds later the owner of those words—the camp commander, who had just entered the mess—raced over to the young boy and crashed a steel chair over his head. It was a serious blow, and we stirred to the defence of the boy, the four of us holding our rifles close.

The recruit, with blood coming from his face, ran out of the building; the camp commander, carrying only a side arm, approached us, apologising profusely about the recruit. Tony gave a short shake of his head, 'No', and we left, our rifles by our sides.

Dust-off

After spending three weeks in the bush with the land-clearing mob, I was glad to be back in Nui Dat where I could take off my boots, get some air around my toes, put on some thongs and walk down to the boozer.

On my way down there I stopped to help some mates who were building a tank stand, and heard the news that my mate Tony—who I'd been working with only the week before—had been hit by an RPG and was in hospital in Vung Tau. No one knew how badly he was hurt, but it didn't sound good.

I was still trying to digest this news as I helped the other four blokes shift one of the tank-stand poles, when one of the blokes slipped on a metal sheet, which then flew out and cut my left foot in half. With two of us down, the pole landed on top of the man who'd slipped. We all scrambled to free him. He was okay.

In shock, I walked back to the path I'd previously been on, hoping to go back in time to when I'd had both feet intact. I kicked my left foot out, as you do when your thong breaks at the front and ends up under your instep. As I looked down, hoping it was just my thong, I noticed a fair amount of blood. Somebody's in trouble, I thought. Then I realised my toes and part of my instep were missing. I soon found them, under the arch of my foot, joined on only by a layer of skin.

My mate ran over and yelled to a medic, then advised me to lie down on the path. I could see now that it was a serious situation, but I couldn't see how to reverse time or back up and take another path to the boozer and avoid this accident. The thought of lying down on the path frightened me, because it would mean I accepted what had happened.

I didn't feel the needle as the medic gave me morphine, and was soon on a stretcher on a jeep heading for the medevac dust-off. I lost track of a few moments, then found myself squinting intermittently at the sun's rays, which were being broken by the rotor of the dust-off chopper. The rotor blade wasn't turning yet, but a slight breeze moved it up and down.

I was all alone. Why had I been deserted here? Turning my head, I could see two VC prisoners to one side, hanging onto a chicken-wire fence with razor wire on top. They did not smile or scorn. I wondered what they felt, looking at me, unarmed and helpless. I looked at their small prison yard and could not see anything they could throw at me. Their expressions were benign. I was no longer a threat to them.

In the tent behind the windbreak I could hear a TV playing *McHale's Navy*. My attempts to throw rocks to gain the pilot's attention failed. When *McHale's Navy* was over he came out, the door gunners loaded me onto the helicopter and we took off for the task force hospital at Vung Tau.

Stainless-steel bedrails

The emotion of being at the hospital was too much: my mouth was dry, my brain seemingly alert yet at the same time numb and warm, as is the way with morphine.

Waiting to be sewn up, I saw my mate Tony through a gap in a curtain in intensive care: no legs, only one arm, and a hand with only one finger. I got my wheelchair alongside his bed. There was a nurse with red eyes on one side and me on the other; we were surrounded by blue plastic curtains.

Once again I could not talk, but there was no one else. The comfort of not talking was not an option. The need for me to offer kind, loving, human attention had never been greater. I was trying to summon every whit of knowledge I had so that somehow I could be of some use.

My eyes ached from trying to grasp and control the situation. Tony said he didn't think it was worth going on. He was frightened that people would make fun of him, like they had of old Tom, a gardener at core training who had suffered mental injuries in the Korean war. Tony said, 'I don't want the army's pity.'

What could I say to a man who only a few days earlier had shown me a picture of his wife and young daughter?

Guilt

After surgery I was wheeled into a ward of twelve beds facing each other. Another dust-off chopper landed as I was being transferred to a bed.

The mood of some of the soldiers there was hard to describe: their humour was childish and uncertain, almost pre-primary school. The war was over for most of us; while our mates were still out there under threat, we were nowhere. We were in an unrecognisable place: proper toilets, white linen on the beds, meals served on plates, and air conditioning. In the space of one short helicopter ride our lives had changed. Our training hadn't prepared us for this.

What about our loyal mates? Why couldn't they go home too? Guilt started to set in. Once again, like on my first day in-country, talking required intense concentration. I could not join in the humour a few soldiers attempted, or talk easily to the more seriously wounded. In the jungle we had loyalty and danger. Now, in hospital, we had white sheets, no work and an uncertain future.

Before I was called up into the army I'd had a very easy life as a deckhand in WA's north-west. So army life had come as a bit of a shock, particularly Vietnam. But when you're twenty years old, all going well, one day just leads to the next. You follow orders and do as you're told, and with any luck things will work out.

The next day I learned about 'happy hour'. Mondays from 1 pm to 2 pm. That's when all the 'brass' and the odd politician visited the hospital. Our directions were to sit up and smile, if we could, and make their tour as pleasant as possible. Answer any questions politely, no smoking, and if you're congratulated for anything, shake hands, if you have them. If not, keep your arms under the white linen—not like some stupid bastard did last week when he held up a stump to a politician. Poor taste indeed.

I was still high on painkillers that first happy hour, and fading in and out of consciousness. That day the tour included Big Malcolm, the Minister for Defence, a brigadier general, two surgeons, the matron, the sheila from the Red Cross and several others. I was a bit nervous. They would be at my bed in a minute. That minute disappeared and those strange people surrounded me.

The surgeon picked up my clipboard and was reading a few things out to Malcolm. Between drifting in and out of consciousness, I heard the doc say, 'This man will be medevaced home to Australia on the next Hercules.' I opened my eyes and felt under attack, with people, who were all out of focus, all around me. I yelled out, 'I'm not fucking going home!' Then, realising what I had just said, I opted for passing out.

The next day when I woke up, the other patients thanked me for brightening up happy hour. I asked the sister if I could visit my mate in intensive care. She got me a wheelchair and in we went.

Tony lifted his head and held up his hand. I gently squeezed his one finger. He asked what had happened to me and how come I was in a wheelchair, and was I going to be all right. I again found it hard to talk. But the emotion of being needed gave me strength, and I listened as he said, 'I'm not much use to anyone now.'

'You still have lots of friends, and we'll all stand by you,' I said. 'Don't worry, mate.'

Seeing him there in this white linen bed with shiny steel sides, I hoped he knew I would always be there for him, and I would not forget.

Panic or peace

The worst I ever feel is when I'm in a hospital—whether as a patient or as a visitor—and when I was in the army hospital in Vung Tau I was both patient and visitor, with what I first thought was a terrible injury.

I later realised I was going to survive, and probably without too much discomfort. But some of the people around me had horrific injuries—in particular my friend Tony, who did not think he could go on living. Legs and arms don't grow back. It was just too hard; the bar was too high.

The week before, we had both been fit and healthy; we were bulletproof, and nothing could harm us. Now, while I was temporarily in a wheelchair, the best Tony might have hoped for was that maybe one day he would be able to sit in one—and that wasn't a thought he could entertain. He spoke as if talking to himself.

I was in that hospital for four days, and apart from the morphine and bandages, I was a visitor. A visitor is someone who is concerned; a patient is someone who, in the midst of a catastrophe, yields to peace and logical inevitability. He talks quietly as his brain protects him from panic; logic calms his fears as his brain narrows his focus until he himself is the only person he is talking to.

The next day, Billy, Lorrie, the Bobs and even Underpants Mervin managed to get a special pass to come down to Vung Tau to bid me farewell. A celebration was called for.

The Red Cross sheila said no to the use of the Red Cross room if beer was going to be involved, and the ward sister said I could only have one visitor at a time.

'So can I sit outside in my wheelchair with me mates, who have come down specially and are waiting outside?' I asked.

'Well, okay,' she said.

Well, one thing led to another, and talk of me being carried in my wheelchair over the sandy hills to the boozer near the beach soon turned into action. It was the funniest thing. It took four strong men to carry me over the sand dunes, and one angry matron to drag me back.

It wasn't until I travelled to Sydney for the official welcome-home parade for Vietnam veterans twenty-five years later that I saw those blokes again.

Departure

The next day I was carried on a stretcher and loaded into a Hercules transporter. It was already after sundown, and much darker inside—like going into a picture theatre late, with all those little lights in the dark interior. But there were no seats—only stretchers everywhere—and I didn't dare ask what was in those long boxes. The RAAF nurse held my hand for a fair while. I guess I was a bit frightened. She said she would like to put me to sleep now. I begged her not to until we were out over the ocean and less likely to be shot down.

I started to make out the shapes around me. I could see that everyone else was asleep. The pilots sat way up the top on these planes—it would take a ten-foot ladder to get up there. I asked if I could climb up there and have a look—a silly request, considering that I was strapped to a stretcher and my left arm and leg were in plaster.

'Where does the plane land?' I asked.

'Butterworth,' she said.

'Is that near Sydney?'

'No, it's in Malaya.'

'Shit! Am I on the right plane?'

'Yes,' she said. 'We refuel and stabilise the patients for a few days, and then take off for Sydney.'

'Oh,' I said. Then she put me to sleep.

July, 3 am

Dark and wet outside, I can hear rain on a tin roof. It's a bit wet where I am as well.

I heard similar noises earlier today, but these are more repetitive. Push, take it easy, then push again.

I know something is going on. Is this the big push? I wonder.

I'm scared. It's so dark that I'm not sure if my eyes are open or closed. I even touch the corner of my eyelids to make sure. I no longer feel secure.

Among this commotion my surroundings are changing and the noises are getting louder. They're the same sort of noises but more urgent. My footing and grip are to no avail. I'm quite anxious now. There's no denying that I am part of what's going on. Will I be able to handle my role? How long will it last? My mouth is dry, the type of dry you get when you confront a scary situation.

There must be others around. But it's so dark that I cannot see.

The avalanche of life is in control. This is something I feel and yet can't explain. My surroundings are closing in; I feel the movement, the intensity now frantic. I'm not in the same place. Will I ever be there again? I'm quite worried now, the pressure is so great. Is this the beginning or the end?

I am naked, no weapon, no protection.

I'm sliding now under great pressure. I feel worried, then, suddenly, no pressure. Everything lights up like a million candlepower. Everything is so bright I don't know where I am. I take a hit on the backside and cry with pain. I start to see people congratulating each other like it's all over. The main sound I can hear now is coming from me, blanketed by the gentle rain on the tin roof of the Leonora District Hospital. The nurse hands me to my mother. Her first son.

Malaya

Butterworth. A hospital on the beach, starched light-blue sheets, a nice open ward, thick green grass for about thirty feet, fifty feet of sand and then the ocean. It all seemed to be on the same level. Can't have much of a tide, I thought.

The man next to me, probably twenty-one years old, was paralysed from the neck down. The man next to him was his co-pilot; he had lower spinal injuries. I had seen their helicopter crash. In fact, I'd been talking to them on the radio when they were shot down.

'Throw smoke.'

'I have thrown smoke.'

'I see purple.'

'Purple is correct,' I'd said. Then they'd disappeared, probably half a mile away. Now we were all in beds with starched light-blue sheets.

We stayed at Butterworth for two or three days. The Red Cross nurse went over to Penang for us to buy duty-free electrical goods and cameras. I bought a big radio. The guy next to me bought a reel-to-reel tape recorder. Our main concern was whether we would get through Customs okay on our return to Australia.

Australia

Sydney. Large beds with starched white linen sheets, windows with curtains pulled back, rays of sunshine streaming through cigarette smoke, basking in the Saturday morning.

A large National radio on the window ledge was tuned in to the horseracing channel. The volume was just loud enough to give atmosphere and yet not intrude.

The crisp early-morning air was beginning to feel familiar. The air itself carried a sense of atmosphere, bedpans clattering, visitors talking, the next race about to start: the weekend had just begun. *You either know what Saturday morning looks like or you don't*, said a voice inside my head.

Nurses, doctors and visitors were all talking quietly, as if we had not heard loud noises before. The bursar was discussing travel arrangements with the guy next to me.

'You'll be fine on the bus,' he was saying. 'Look, you can call your parents and let them know what time you'll arrive in Adelaide, and they can help you off the bus. It's not that far. Just make sure you go to the toilet before you get on the bus.'

It was still early, but you only had to open your eyes, if you had 'em, to see that it was Saturday morning. This special Saturday morning feeling only lasted for about an hour, and then it felt like the last day of boarding school.

The bursar signed a clipboard and turned in my direction. I looked out the window. The dog lying in the sun on the footpath outside had had enough early-morning sunshine and decided to move. The bursar pulled his chair up to my bed and said, 'G'day.' I suddenly realised that I hadn't spoken a word since arriving in Australia, and was happy not to be involved with all these people. They seemed strange and removed and could only upset my dream world.

He looked at my clipboard. The silence was mounting. He must know I could talk.

'G'day,' I said reluctantly.

We looked at each other with about the same lack of interest—he who had a job to do, and me who just wanted to know what was going to happen next.

'Can you board a plane using crutches?' he asked me.

'My left leg and arm are in plaster, my right foot is bandaged, and I keep losing track of where I am every time the sister gives me a needle,' I said. 'Apart from that, I'll fly the bloody thing home if you like.'

'If we send you home on a stretcher, the domestic airlines insist on putting a curtain around you and closing off half of first class. That's twelve seats. Other passengers don't like to see someone in a stressful situation. It doesn't do us much good either—it's bad publicity. Now, if you can manage to use crutches and sit up, we'll try to get you home to Perth as soon as possible.'

'I don't even have a uniform,' I said.

'Don't worry. We'll fix all that up.'

'GP boots,' I said. 'Not them old hard leather ones.'

'You can't even wear boots.'

'You got me there.'

'You'll have the same nice first lieutenant nurse to escort you.'

'That'll be fine,' I said. I remembered her from the hospital at Vung Tau. She was the sister who'd got caught on the pathway one night in between wards, wrapped around the young surgeon, when someone had tripped a flare and everything had lit up.

Pig's bum

It was nice to lean on someone, getting onto the plane. I wondered if she knew I noticed her. It didn't really matter.

We hardly spoke a word on the flight over. She gave me some pills. I was feeling calm and relaxed. It had been a while since I'd sat next to a woman, especially an attractive one with nice legs. For a fleeting moment I thought maybe my hand could slip off the armrest and end up resting on her leg.

I wondered if anyone else knew who I was—in fact, was I anyone?

We arrived in Perth at 11.30 pm. 'We'll be the last to get off,' the nurse said, and by the time we'd made it to the gangway the floodlights on the tarmac had been turned off. There was a misty rain, and the hostesses had already made a dash for the passenger terminal.

My friend in uniform helped me down the stairs. No one was clapping or cheering like when we'd left. Three of my sisters were standing by the fence in the rain.

'Are you all right?' one called out. 'You had us worried. How come you're walking? Were you shot? The army chaplain said it was serious.'

No time for family contact. My sisters were left standing there as I was helped into the waiting army ambulance. I felt, for a minute, that I might be important after all.

I lay down for the trip from the airport to the veterans'

hospital, but sat up on arrival. The driver got out and rang the after-hours bell. The place looked a bit dark and scary, but I remembered being there with my dad visiting one of his mates a long time ago, and that made me feel a little more comfortable.

Thirty seconds later he rang the bell again. This time a big woman, the matron, answered the big dark door.

'Transfer of wounded patient to veterans' hospital,' the driver said, and presented the paperwork.

'Pig's bum,' the matron replied. 'Not at this hour, you don't.'

'But you have to!'

'No, I don't.'

'Yes, you do! This man has just returned from active service with terrible injuries, and this is the veterans' hospital. You have to accept him!'

'Pig's bum. Not at this hour on a Sunday night. Bring him back with all your paperwork on Monday morning. Admissions are 8 am to 4 pm.'

'Where to now?' the driver asked the nurse, who was still looking after me.

'We'll have to take him to Campbell Barracks,' she said. 'They have a twenty-four hour staffed first aid post. We can't take him anywhere else; the press would have a field day if they found out that the veterans hospital wouldn't admit him because it was late at night.'

She turned to me and said, 'It's just a shed on a hill, but there are staff on hand, and they're equipped to look after bed patients. It will have to do until we can take you back to Hollywood on Monday morning.' She opened her bag.

I said, 'I'm okay, I don't need a needle.'

She pretended not to hear me.

'You'd better hang on,' she said. 'It's going to be a bumpy ride.'

Red cheeks

G Ward was one big room with twenty-four patients in it. It was partitioned into six sections by a waist-high wall topped with a panel of glass that brought the height of the wall up to that of a very short man. There were curtains that could be pulled around each bed for extra privacy.

Each section contained four patients. Each patient had a bed and a stainless-steel bedside cupboard with a jug of water, a glass and an ashtray on top. Some of the older patients regularly had fresh flowers in a vase. One old bloke who never had any visitors also often had flowers. This was attributed to the Red Cross woman who was friends with the woman who ran the kiosk in the hallway.

Most of the men were ex-soldiers from World War II. One was from the Korean conflict, and then there was me and another fellow from the Vietnam police action—or 'conflict', as one of the old blokes put it. He didn't think us young kids should be in the veterans' hospital. He said it just didn't seem right: Hollywood Repatriation Hospital was for war veterans. The bloke from the Korean conflict looked over sympathetically and said, 'Don't worry about him, mate.'

The other Vietnam bloke was missing his right leg, and depended on a wheelchair to get around. When he pulled up alongside my bed I recognised his cheeky grin. His injury hadn't caught up with his confidence. We were bulletproof, and at an age when fit men could piss from the highest mountain.

He reached out to shake my hand, smiled, made strong contact and never blinked once. He was trying to hold firm his emotions. He said he had had enough of the army and would be glad when his two years of National Service was over and he could go back to his civilian life. Looking at his red cheeks, I knew that he knew he was just marching time. He was a brave man: he didn't hesitate to talk about his situation, and when it looked like there might be some emotional stumbling block, he talked faster and his cheeks got redder.

The hospital was well run. Our ward had several nurses, including the head nurse, who everyone called Sister. The nurses all wore white dresses with funny-looking white caps that didn't seem to have any purpose. There were also nurses' aides, who wore light-pink dresses. The tea lady and a religious woman came around every day with smiles, cake and pamphlets; they were very friendly and you couldn't help but smile back. Cleaners in khaki came every day and mopped and polished the floors, wiped the windows and emptied the ashtrays.

On each side of the ward were windows that were about twenty feet from the windows of the next ward. Outside, against the red brick walls, were gardens of gladiolas, hydrangeas and other plants popular in the sixties—there may have been hibiscus and boronia shrubs, too. Every day we'd see the gardeners out there weeding or pruning. In between the gardens was a long strip of lawn about ten feet wide, and at first light every morning the sprinklers would come on. That was about the time the first man awake lit up a cigarette. Smoke often filled the air, and I didn't object much, but we sure could have done with the two-can beer ration we had in the army hospital at Vung Tau.

Visiting hours were between six and eight, and my sister Trish called in each day after work and smuggled in two cold cans of beer in her handbag. On weekends she smuggled in six cold cans in an esky that was decorated with Christmas wrapping paper and made to look like a woman's handbag—it fitted neatly into my bedside cupboard. I had a protective canopy over my legs like a small tent, which was a good place to quietly open a can of beer. When Trish came back to visit on the Monday she would always joke, 'Oh, that's where I left my handbag!'

Trish was great in that time of undisclosed stress; she was my link between being bulletproof and naked. The nurses were friendly, too. Although it was a veterans' hospital, it was staffed by civilians. This made it a bit like a halfway house: talking and joking with Australian civilian nurses was the first step in our reassimilation into Australian society—but just as you got to know them, the wicked hospital matron would change the roster and send them to different wards. Getting a sponge bath from a new nurse was plain scary. If something went wrong, I could be up on a charge of conduct to the prejudice of good army discipline, or perhaps an accidental discharge in a non-combat zone.

Nighttimes were the worst, with the old blokes snoring and having other problems that the night sister would have to attend to. I started to agree with the grumpy old bloke who'd said that us kids shouldn't be there.

One sock too many

My friend in the wheelchair told me he'd only been in Vietnam for three weeks when an RPG had taken his leg off. He was lucky to be alive.

Every now and then he and a one-armed friend from another ward would sneak out and go to the local pub. The publican was a good bloke who even bought them a few drinks. Getting back into the hospital was the hard part.

My friend offered to organise some crutches for me so I could come along. We would have to make sure the sister didn't catch us, though, because she could get really pissed off and had previously threatened to tell Matron.

'Perhaps after my next operation,' I said.

That same second-rate doctor from Vung Tau ended up operating on my foot a second time, and when I first came to I heard him say to the nurse that I was lucky. They'd saved my foot, but my toes would always be numb and I would have some discomfort. He also said I would be in line for a small pension. I felt insulted that this doctor thought everything would be all right because I could get a small pension. My eyes were half open, and my capacity to think was at a similar level; the obscenities that warmed my eyes remained in my head.

The sergeant major from the Karrakatta army base often called in to say hello. He asked me to keep an eye on my one-legged friend, as he was causing a few problems—particularly when the nurses changed his dressings. He had no qualms, he said, about showing off his private parts in front of the nurses. He had been a shy boy when he'd first come here, but he'd soon lost his inhibitions; he'd even made one young nurse, who had probably never seen an erection before, run to the sister in tears.

Lying in a hospital bed, one tends to be a bit more outspoken and a little less afraid of people with high rank. I suggested that, having had his whole bloody leg blown off, and his private parts being right next to where his leg used to be, it would be a bit difficult when they were dressing his almost nonexistent stump for him not to expose himself. He was probably just counting his blessings that certain parts of his body were still working.

When they gave me a set of crutches to get around on, I started to feel a little better. It would soon be Christmas, when the hospital would cut staff numbers for the holidays. The doctors would approve leave for those of us who could walk and had family to look after them.

I told the nurse in charge that my oldest sister was a triple-certificate-trained nursing sister. I didn't mention that she was living in New Guinea.

And so, wearing army pyjamas and an army dressing gown, and with the help of my sister Trish, I hobbled out of the hospital on Christmas leave.

Home

Home didn't feel the same. The walls, the roof, the floor all looked the same, and the picture on the fridge of me as a boy in a fancy-dress costume holding a cardboard sword looked real, but I felt differently towards all these things. They couldn't offer me the protection they once had. Life wasn't that simple any more. I was wearing somebody else's clothes, for fuck's sake.

The next day, with the aid of crutches, my sister Sue and I walked to our local shops. People I should have felt comfortable seeing made my cheeks flush.

'What happened to you? Did you get shot? Did you shoot any of them?'

'No,' I said, 'but I did help build a windmill.'

There was John, working on his Austin A40, greasy hands and Elvis Presley hair. He didn't come out to say g'day to his long-time friend, and it was probably just as well. I felt so far removed that I could hardly manage a 'How ya goin?'

I realised at that moment that my brain needed liberating from conformity—and not just army conformity, either. From now on I would consider my options from a lateral point of view, and nothing would be out of the question.

I would have a change of lifestyle when my two years was up in October. Perhaps I'd grow long hair and a beard, put patches on my jeans, become a hippie and travel the world.

Although I wasn't sure what a hippie was, I thought it might be a positive change—and the controversy it would cause in my neighbourhood would probably be a good thing, too.

Big bang theory

I'm not sure that anyone knows the answer. One minute it's there; the next, bang, it's not. It happens so quick you wonder if it was ever there.

With big things, like a French-colonial concrete bridge spanning a river in Vietnam, there is, of course, a residual concrete rubbish dump of French-colonial importance, as well as the visual distress and the ringing in the ears that stays with you forever.

But with small things, like a bomb, when the dust clears there's nothing but a hole in the ground, and you have to start wondering about the theory of creation. Like who created that hole, and what was its purpose, and who's in charge, and why does the person in charge allow people to get their legs blown off?

I hate hospitals and needles and stainless-steel beds. Who created the need for such things? And when did all this disrespect start?

Apparently, in the beginning there was a word. Some say the word was 'bust', as in 'busting' or 'I'll bust you down to a private'. Or, if you came from Kentucky, 'I'll bust you upside the head'. Or in Perth, down on the beach, one might say, 'Nice bust'.

The next lot of words, according to my old mate Jerry who

drove a grader for the council, was two words: 'Thank you', as in 'thank you for the nice bust', or 'Thank you for the pit stop; I was busting' or, of course, 'Thank you for slowing down and stopping'.

Incidentally, 'slow' and 'stop' came from my mate Trevor, who was a signal man for the main roads repair crew. Nice work, Trev. The courtesy you have displayed towards your fellow man is admiral.

All the other words just followed on, like 'creation'.

For instance, 'By crikey, that's a nice creation'.

Dingbat

A small addendum, or a modest understanding of a life personified by friendship.

Now that my mate has taken up with that dingbat sheila down by the pines, things have changed. I told him not to do it, but what can you do? Man needs woman, and perhaps his need is greater than I understand. They both strive to show how ordinary they are, to gain trust and skin-deep friendship with each other. They're a two-person team striving for social acceptance.

I've seen it happen before. A fellow has his way with a sheila and then ducks out the back to see his mates to make sure he's still normal before she starts knitting or needs a cup of tea in bed.

He was a sweet talker, Trevor, a little shallow, a little narrow, even trustworthy, but on the shallow, narrow side, a pleasant fellow all the same. He worked hard at defining his demeanour.

'I'm going to marry her,' he said.

'Don't be silly,' I said. 'She screams like a dingbat. She keeps cats. I hate cats, as you know, for all the death they cause to the native wildlife.'

'She owns a house,' he said. 'She keeps it tidy and she knows how to please a man.'

'That sort of pleasure is one thing, all right, but don't you ever want to undo the chains of "modest understanding", the chains of conformity? Break the chains, set the bar a little higher until you feel the blood in your veins tingle with excitement? Be a little adventurous, try honesty? Have faith in something more than just survival?'

That was the last I saw of Trevor. I don't really miss him that much. It was a bit like losing one of the TV channels.

Mr. Arthur E. George,

Dampier Mining,

KOOLAN ISLAND, W. A., 6733.

Registration No. 5009769

After

CALL-UP

You are hereby called up for service in the Military Forces of the Commonwealth.

You are required to present

This notice should be presented together with your Certificate of Registration when reporting for service.

Enclosed are travel warrants to cover your journey from Koolan Island to Derby, Derby to Port Hedland and finally Port Hedland to Perth. Departure times are: MMA flight will depart Koolan Island at 1.30 p.m. on 30th September, 1968 which will be followed by your boarding at MMA flight 464 at Derby at 3.00 p.m. on 30th September, 1968. At Port Hedland you will depart via Ansett ANA flight 252 at 12.45 p.m. on 1st October, 1968. On arrival in Perth on presentation of the warrants you will be supplied with rail

Let's join the RSL

Suddenly, with the signing of a piece of paper, we were no longer soldiers. There was a great sense of emptiness; a lack of direction. After two years in the army, discharge day was more confusing than our first day. What to do? Where to go? We sought solace in the pub. Drink was often our friend, as one day seemed the same as the next. Then my mate Buj suggested we join the Returned Services League.

The RSL building stood proud: a long single-storey tin-roofed building on St Georges Terrace in the city. From the footpath you couldn't see the landing at the top of the eight white cement steps that added to its temple-like facade, along with the great big doors, one slightly open. This was the returned soldier's Holy Grail. We had been taught as children to respect the RSL; now we were going to climb those steps ourselves and apply for membership.

Buj and I climbed the steps and looked inside the half-open door. There was a large wooden dance floor with a stage at one end, with a small office on each side.

An elderly gentleman in a dark suit and tie, with an RSL badge on his lapel, greeted us: 'Can I help you?'

We immediately felt like we should have worn civilian clothes instead of these old army greens and black boots.

'Yes,' I said. 'We'd like to join the RSL.'

He looked perplexed. He was obviously a nice old man,

with good manners and grace. He sighed, and smiled: 'Come in and take a seat.'

We sat down like students in the headmaster's office, and he explained: 'The Returned Services League of Australia is for veterans of foreign wars.'

I interrupted him: 'We've just returned from Vietnam.'

'Yes, well, that's not a declared war, it's a police action,' he said. 'However, you may be considered for associated membership if you can find someone to nominate and second your application. Of course, you wouldn't have voting rights.'

'Why can't we be full members?'

'Well, like I said, the RSL is for returned servicemen who have fought in a war on foreign soil.'

I looked up at the picture on the wall of the Queen of England, and at the words underneath it: 'Queen of Australia'. I felt a bit embarrassed. I'd grown up with pictures of the Queen and with her influence—as a child at school I'd even sung 'God Save the Queen'—but Buj was from Poland, and he thought the whole Queen thing was even stranger than I did.

We were both starting to get annoyed and frustrated with this nice old man who smiled and sighed a lot but didn't understand that we wanted recognition of our National Service; recognition of the fact that our lives had changed and of the fact that our pre-army friends seemed strange and even untrustworthy. We'd been part of a team based on loyalty and trust, a team that had grown and matured in an inexplicable direction. Our pre-army friends still smiled just the same as before, but their smiles were now foreign to us. The bridge to their friendship was not secured. An invisible danger existed, with no perimeter defence. No one seemed to understand, not even this old man who must have been nearly sixty and had probably been welcomed home with a street parade when he'd returned from active duty.

'We need to join the RSL,' Buj said, 'and we would like to fill out an application form for full membership right now.'

Just then another old gentleman turned up, also wearing a dark suit and with an RSL badge on his lapel. He said he'd overheard our conversation from the other office, and that he believed some RSL branches were now accepting Vietnam veterans as full members.

The situation was embarrassing. With red faces, we filled out the forms to join. Then we left and headed for the pub and didn't go back to the RSL for twenty-five years—that's when the government held an official welcome-home parade for Vietnam veterans.

Me and Buj

Everyone in the army called him Buj. His full name is Joe Bujnowski—Joe is short for the Polish name Jerzy. He answers the phone 'Joe Buj'.

After the army we took a year and travelled around Australia, and I started calling him Joseph. Nowadays I call him Joe—except when I greet him on the phone, when I still call him Joseph.

Our trip around Australia was a fun time. The only clothes we had were army greens. I don't know what had happened to our civilian clothes—perhaps they didn't fit us any more, after two years, or more likely they seemed strange and untrustworthy. Either way, we loaded our greens and our boots into Buj's Ford Zephyr and took off. Maybe we would travel north where it was nice and warm, find a cave that was stacked full of beer, with a cool freshwater spring. Outside the cave there would be a white sandy beach with clear blue water with fish for the taking, our security protected by thick inland jungle.

We each had a sleeping bag, and we shared a large faded blue tarpaulin, generally folded over us, for protection both from the ground and from possible rain. We would drive until we got tired—it didn't matter where we were—then just stop and throw the tarp down and go to sleep.

One night when we were sleeping in a tiny park in the

middle of Adelaide at about 2 am, a police paddy wagon pulled up and stopped. Its blue light went on. Two young cops came over and said, 'Hey fellas, you can't sleep here.'

Buj rolled over in his sleeping bag, produced a machete, and told them to bugger off, which they did. I never really understood why they did, but they surely did.

Buj had a way about him. It was never what he said; it was how he said it. Like when he told those two cops to bugger off—they must have thought it was the sensible thing to do. He is still a legend today.

I was talking to an old army mate, Mick Vanpoteren, the other day when out of the blue he said, 'Remember when Buj put that corporal in his place? He said, "There's only one fool around here, and you're both of them." He said it with such conviction and confidence that the corporal walked away a shaken man.'

We tended to favour small country towns, even if it was just for one night, with a few beers and a game of darts at the local pub. On those formal occasions Buj always wrote my name on the scoreboard as '½A'—short for Arthur. My real name is Ted; that's short for Edward. On official papers it's Arthur Edward, but I sign them 'Ted'. My last name might only confuse the situation: Buj sometimes calls me Mr George.

In the twelve months we travelled around Australia, we never once talked about the war. We both had full beards, so if it hadn't been for the army clothes and our reluctance to talk about the war, we might have been thought of as hippies and not been afforded the hospitality of the country people. We were often asked in little outback pubs, when the locals saw us in army greens, whether we'd been 'over there'.

To us the war had no beginning or end. We didn't go as a unit or come home as a unit. We were all staggered, individual replacement soldiers. We left in the night and twelve months later we returned in the night, generally around three in the morning.

On most Tuesdays one or two REOs from our unit would go home, having completed their twelve months' tour of duty on active service. On most Thursdays one or two new REOs would take their place, with 365 days to go until they woke up in Australia again. For them the countdown had just begun.

In our unit everyone knew how many days they had to go. Three hundred and sixty-five days was a long time, and thirty days or less was a short time. When you were 'short time' you yelled it out as often as possible: 'Thirty and a wakie!' When you got down to 'one and a wakie' you knew that the next time you woke up you would be in Australia.

The war had started seven years before I'd got there and apparently finished two years after I left. It was still going on while Buj and I were travelling around Australia. But I don't think wars are ever over for those who serve in them.

The golden hair

Halfway around Australia we came to Townsville, and found work on a large fishing boat that was preparing for the prawn season in the Gulf of Carpentaria. Buj was employed as third engineer and I was a deckhand. The ship was over five hundred tons and had a crew of twenty-eight—half male and half the other sort.

The captain's name was Don, but you used it at your peril. 'Captain or Sir,' he said. Calling him Sir didn't bother me. I'd got used to calling people Sir in the army, and before that at high school; all the teachers had had to be called Sir and I'd hated nearly all of them, so calling this man Sir was a piece of cake. Everyone disliked him, particularly the women, who nicknamed him 'the wolf in long white socks'.

The bosun's name was Tim, and he was a simple man with skills exceeding most. He was thin like a snake, but fast like Speedy Gonzales. He was an ex–Golden Gloves boxer and his hands hung off his skinny arms, motionless, waiting for a command. His body was calm even though he had a high-pitched voice. His eyes were the only part of him that showed emotion.

One day the captain sent Taffy, the Welsh guy, up the crow's nest. His job was to look for disturbances in the water, which indicated prawns. Tim looked up and realised there was something wrong about the way Taffy was hugging the mast.

Tim jumped down from the fishing deck, landing on the foredeck running, and within seconds was up the mast like a spider and had wrapped his long skinny arms around Taffy and the mast rail. They stayed there for some time, then slowly climbed down. All the time Tim had his arms completely around Taffy and the mast rail, as they descended one step at a time. Shaking as he walked, we took Taffy below to his bunk. He eventually told us he was scared of heights. Tim's eyes watered, as he knew he had done a wonderful thing.

Perry had a bunk next to mine. He was a Yank, from California. He'd served in the funny farm too, over there in the war, as a second lieutenant in General Custer's old outfit, the 7th Cav.

He didn't talk much; nor did his girlfriend. In fact, she talked so little she was only known as Perry's girlfriend. She was a thin blonde with pale silky hair on her upper lip and under her ears—although, come to think of it, the hair under her ears was lighter and fine, like a web a small spider would make.

Perry eventually moved out from the bunk next to me to live with his girlfriend on the top deck in a caravan.

One day, with the sun just starting to set, I got a good close look at that hair around Perry's girlfriend's ears. She was between the sun and me, obviously a lot closer to me than the sun; probably a bit too close. Nothing else seemed to be in focus. She said, 'I wish a pox on the captain.'

Tim, who was sewing a net with me, looked at Horse. Horse looked at me, and I looked at Perry, who seemed to know what she was talking about. The rest of us weren't sure. Tim, the bosun, thought he did, and cast his mind about for a sexual connotation, then realised that a sexual connotation involving pox was a bit over the top, even for him.

She stood there, protecting me from the glare of the evening sun. I lowered my eyes to regain focus, but all I could see was one magnificent full-bodied golden hair on her suntanned thigh, surrounded with a shine like a halo. This one hair was in the company of a few smaller less significant pale hairs, which lay flat to her skin like they were paying homage to that one golden hair. It was magnificent, a good half-inch long, paling at the tip but sparkling along its entire length like a strobe light with a tinge of red from the sun. It was slightly curved like half a rainbow, but pointy at the tip and with a substantial girth where it grew from her suntanned thigh.

I turned to Perry and said, 'Do you want to fight?'

He said, 'Sure,' as you would expect under those circumstances, so we went to the top deck behind the caravan.

The customary formalities completed, we moved to within striking range.

Just then, the ship's bell was rung. It was the cook, giving out the daily two-can beer ration. Perry gave me one of his cans, and we became shipmates.

Margaret was the ship's first officer, radio operator and first aid officer. She was a very competent and compassionate person who had recently been discharged from the Australian Army as a second lieutenant at only twenty-three.

Her cabin and radio room was next to the captain's cabin. One third of her cabin space was the radio room; divided by a curtain, the other two-thirds was her small bedroom, which included a sink where she kept her first-aid stuff. One day while she was doing some first aid on my finger, the captain walked into the radio room and then straight into her bedroom, and saw me with my back to him and my hands out in front of me.

'What's going on here?' he said.

I turned, holding a bowl of disinfectant in one hand and revealing a half-bandaged finger on the other.

'Oh,' he said, and left.

Margaret looked at me, smiled and said nothing, as very competent people do sometimes.

The poet

Bill, the cook—also known as Cookie—had lived in the bush all his life. He couldn't read or write, but he could recite off by heart poetry that he'd learnt around bush campfires.

Some evenings, if we were at anchor and someone had smuggled some extra beer on board, a group of us would go to the top deck and get comfortable among the fishing nets, and Bill would start reciting poetry. He was a bit like a preacher the way he held us together. He must have been at least sixty years old, and although we didn't have a campfire, his face shone like there was one.

The first time I went up there it was pitch black, but if you looked forward you could see the anchor light on the bow mast. Cookie recited his favourite poem, 'My Brother Ben and I'. It seemed to go on for hours, verse after verse. I had a suspicion that he was making some of it up just so he could carry on reciting poetry all night, but it didn't really matter as there wasn't much else to do. The only time he stopped was to take a drink or have a burp. He didn't even stop when he leant over the side.

Bill was very keen on alcohol. I'd heard him tell the captain that he couldn't cook on two cans a day. He needed twelve, he'd always had twelve, and if he didn't get twelve he wasn't going to cook.

Foo, the first engineer, was a lovely round man from Singapore. He'd signed on for the trip from England to

Australia, expecting to be flown home to Singapore when that journey was over, but the captain wouldn't let him go until a replacement was found. Foo was classified as an illegal immigrant, and could be arrested if he stepped off the ship; the ship's captain and owners would also most likely get heavy fines. This worried the captain a lot, because every time Foo had a chance he would take a stroll along the quiet beach, away from the noisy engine room. The captain had told Foo not to go ashore, and he'd told me that if he did, I had to go with him and make sure he didn't talk to anyone. Most importantly, I was to make sure he came back to the ship.

Foo was a kind and generous man who shared his beer ration and cooked treats like fried octopus in soy sauce. Although he didn't speak English, he communicated with us well with gestures and smiles. He showed me a photo of his wife and children and the very small apartment they lived in. Foo wanted to go back home to them to Singapore but the captain wouldn't let him. I thought of other times in history when a bad captain had gone missing, presumed washed overboard and never heard of again ... But we were all pretty nice people.

Then there was Doug, from Canada. I asked him once if you spelt Canada with a capital 'C'. We got along pretty well. He was the second engineer and always wore white overalls. His main focus back then in 1971 was to organise a reunion at the Tokyo railway station for New Year's Eve 2000. He really wanted to be a hippie but he was stuck in those white overalls.

There were also two young girls from Thursday Island, but they had to be put off when their religious leader came on board and complained that they were only sixteen years old. The captain was upset that this man had got on board his ship and was interfering with his crew structure by demanding that the girls be put off. The girls were giggly native Islanders, but the religious man was a well-dressed white man carrying a big black book. He had invaded their peaceful island when they were children, under the guise of being a missionary who could lead them to life ever after. It seemed that he wanted everyone to be just like him. He didn't have to think any more: he'd stopped asking the hard questions. He said the answers to all of life's questions were in the book.

Karen and Georgina were from Germany. They were pretty hopeless at heading prawns; their main interest was getting a suntan. They treated Australia like most Australians treat Europe when they're on a working holiday. I'd never thought of it that way before.

The Japanese girl, Keri, giggled and laughed a lot. She didn't speak English either, but she was sharp as a tack when it came to weighing in the prawns she'd headed. She was the number-two header, and wanted to be number one. It was more than just the money; there was pride involved.

The number-one header was Red, a plump fiery redhead from New Zealand, and if there was going to be a problem or a fight then hers was the side you'd want to be on.

Horse came from Sweden, and she was so strong that Tim made her a deckhand. Her boyfriend, Leif, was from Norway. I don't think I ever heard him speak.

With a few more girls from New Zealand and a few from England, we came from a total of thirteen different countries.

Seafarers

We trawled for prawns and also bought prawns from the smaller boats. We processed these, heading and snap freezing them, then packed and stored them in our large freezer. When our main freezer was full, which took about four or five weeks, a freezer ship from Japan would come alongside and we would unload onto it. We would work all day and all night and then, when the job was done, the Japanese crew would come over to our ship for drinks. Then we would go over to their ship and drink some more.

The language barrier didn't seem to matter.

One of their favourite party games was knee-wrestling. It was a formal affair, with introductions like we were at Madison Square Garden rather than in the galley of a Japanese ship in the Gulf of Carpentaria. Hoshimoto would pretend he had a microphone, and announce: 'From Austraalee, introducing Number-One Champion, Tad, and from Japan, introducing Honourable Number-One Champion, Isamu. The referee is honourable Mr Yukio.'

The game was a bit like arm-wrestling, but with knees. The two contestants would get up on the galley table and crouch, left knee on the table, right knee against right knee, arms folded, backs straight. Mr Yukio would give the signal for the game to begin. It was equally a matter of balance, strength and timing. The Japanese were good hosts, offering lots of Suntory whisky and rice wine. They were from one culture and we were from many, but there was a common bond of people working on the ocean.

Our two ships, which were of similar height and length, were tied together and shared the one anchor. The gunwales were cushioned with tyres. The ships groaned and creaked through the night—they had their own language—as us seafaring people groaned and puffed in our own language on the galley table.

In the morning rain the ships groaned no more, as we eased on the winches and released the bollards and waved goodbye, as seafarers do.

The mutiny

Tim looked excited as he rounded up the deckhands. He said, 'We've just received a cyclone warning. Anchor crew, take your positions. The captain has set a course for Mornington Island.' Tim was relishing the drama.

'I guess it's my turn down the chain locker,' I said. That was one job I didn't like.

It took three people to weigh the anchor: one on the winch; one on the hose, washing the mud off the chain; and one down the chain locker, a dark dirty wet hole in the bow.

You wouldn't want to be claustrophobic down there. There was only one way in and one way out, and if you didn't stack the chain properly as it was lowered into the locker, you could easily block off your only exit. Even worse, if you didn't keep moving your feet to stay on top of the ever-mounting chain, you could get trapped under those huge chain links. There was no light, it was wet and it smelt of seaweed, mud and fish. It was also noisy, very noisy. Screams could not be heard. That's how the bosun introduced me to the chain locker.

The average depth in the Gulf of Carpentaria is only six fathoms, or about eleven metres, which means that even in a cyclone we wouldn't get seas like in the big oceans. A North Sea trawler is made for big seas, so it was kind of fun playing cat and mouse with a cyclone. As the day progressed the winds picked up, and by late afternoon the cook couldn't keep food on the stove.

The captain changed direction to try and head out of the storm, as was the standard procedure. A cyclone is an intense low-pressure system, which travels in a clockwise direction, so if you keep the wind on your port side then you're heading away from the eye. We outran the cyclone on the first day, but by the next day it had somehow surrounded us.

Everything had to be tied down, and it was dangerous to be on deck. The best view was from the wheelhouse.

We were going half-speed ahead into white water, waves crashing over the port bow. It was a trade-off, as we really wanted the wind full on our port side to head away from the eye, but we also wanted to head into the wind to keep the ship stable, so the captain chose a 45-degree angle. We had to show respect for who was boss; even the captain respected the ocean.

Les, the oldest deckhand, pointed out the picket fence; that's the uneven horizon caused by big swells. The whole thing was very exciting. It was one of those events that bond people together—all except the captain.

The next morning life had calmed down a bit. The galley was useable again, albeit ankle-deep in condiments, broken plates, pots and pans.

Tim was organising work parties for the clean-up. Malcolm, the deckhand from New Zealand, said he was seasick and was going back to bed after breakfast. The captain, who was walking by, heard this and said, 'No work, no food.'

Malcolm put his hands around his breakfast plate as if to protect it. The captain stepped into the galley and swung his hand across the table, knocking food and hot tea all over the place. Malcolm saw red and took a swing at the captain, who looked at me and said, 'Tie this man up. Take him below and lock him up.'

I stood there, dumbfounded, and said, 'Take him below where, Sir?'

The captain turned to my mate, Joe, and said, 'You help him.'

'We don't have a lock-up,' Joe said.

'Mutiny!' the captain screamed, and headed for the steps to the wheelhouse. 'Mutiny!' he yelled. 'Margaret, we have a mutiny!'

Concerned, Tim and I followed him to the wheelhouse. He went into the radio room and said to Margaret, 'Call the Commonwealth police and report a mutiny!'

Margaret knew from the tone of his voice that we had a problem. She noticed us over his shoulder and acknowledged our presence. The captain turned and ordered us from the bridge and said if we didn't go he would shoot us. Margaret gave us a little nod that he didn't see.

We returned to the galley, where most of the crew had assembled, crammed in like sheep in fear of a fox. Margaret came down a short time later and with a smile told us that the captain was 'having a little lie-down', but not before he'd made her radio in a mutiny call. The police radio operator at the other end had said, 'You're in luck. There's just enough room to put this in the Marine Records, on the same page as the mutiny on the *Bounty*.' Margaret's grin eased the tension.

The captain had also placed a call to London and Townsville, but hadn't managed to get through. He was gibbering about sacking everyone. 'He is not a well man,' Margaret said.

The Irishman's picnic

We sat at anchor for a couple of days, and then a small boat turned up with our new first engineer. Foo was so excited: his bags were packed and he was on that little shuttle boat in no time.

The new first engineer was a small Irish guy. The first thing he said when he got on board was that he would like to organise a picnic, perhaps on one of those sandy little beaches he'd seen on his trip out here.

The captain was flabbergasted. He told the new first engineer that this was a work ship, not a cruise ship. The small Irishman said stubbornly, 'Nonetheless, we will have a picnic, or the ship stays at anchor.'

The captain's lips started to tremble. He was losing control. He put his hands to his sides like he was reaching for his guns, and then to his ears like he was trying to block out this crazy talk of a picnic.

'Seamus is the name,' continued the Irishman. 'My cabin, if you please.'

When we got to his cabin I explained that we'd had a bit of a mutiny the other day and that I'd heard that the captain planned on sacking the rest of the crew.

'Nonsense,' he said. 'I won't stand for it. I'll talk to him tomorrow after the picnic. What beer ration are you on here?'

'Two cans,' I said. 'Except the cook—he's on twelve. He says he's always been on twelve.'

'I'll have the crew's ration brought up to four,' Seamus said. 'Now go and see if you can round up some bats and balls for the picnic.'

Sure enough, nearly the whole crew went on a picnic the very next day. Seamus managed to get extra beer. We had a barbecue and played beach games, and had a fantastic time. The crew from one of the small boats joined in. Margaret was a bit keen on the skipper of that small boat, and hand in hand they disappeared down the beach. It was such an isolated spot that they could have walked for five hundred miles and not seen a soul.

Bill, the cook, liked to be introduced as if Cook was his last name. One of the girls called him Billy le Cook, but I think that went straight over his head. He stood on the beach next to the fire and started reciting poetry.

We ate our food, drank our beer and watched the fire die down; we stayed close together, a small clump of people on a vast white beach.

Margaret came up behind me with her new friend just when it was time to go back to the ship. She whispered in my ear that she was going to spend the night on the small boat, and that if the captain said anything to tell him she'd be back in the morning.

The captain had not had a good week. He positively frothed at the mouth when I told him where she was. He was a repulsive man—all the women hated 'the wolf'—and whenever he came on the main deck I used to howl until he retreated from the bosun's deck. The girls loved this. This was our deck, and the bosun was boss of the deck.

The next day, quite early, Margaret snuck back on board.

I spoke to her that lunchtime. She said she didn't know how the captain was going to take the news that the new first engineer, although highly qualified, had in fact escaped from a mental hospital where he had been an involuntary patient.

The captain's map

Four new fishermen arrived after lunch, flown in from our home port of Townsville, equipped with new wet-weather gear and fishing boots. They'd been picked up at Normanton, down the bottom of the Gulf, and transported to our ship. After they'd met the captain, they casually announced that they'd changed their minds about working on this ship and they wanted to get off.

The captain was stuttering as he went to his cabin; he did not look well at all. Tim, who had a way with words, suggested that they were bushwhackers who had never intended to work on our ship—they'd probably just wanted to catch a free trip to the Gulf, get decked out and then work on one of the smaller boats.

The four men stood on the foredeck with their bags. They looked a bit like they'd just robbed a bank and needed a cigarette. A short time later a medium-sized boat came alongside as if prearranged. All four men jumped on; the boat didn't even tie up.

Early the next morning the captain started sacking people. He could only sack six at a time, as that's how many the small charter plane could hold. The first six were me, Joe, Malcolm, Margaret, and Karen and Georgina from Germany. We were given five minutes' warning to pack our bags and be on the shuttle boat; we were being returned to our home port of Townsville, as maritime law required.

The shuttle boat driver was to take us to the runway at the Aboriginal station about twenty miles inland. We were to go up the Mitchell River, which was tidal and had many branches. The captain drew a map for him, and gave him directions: 'At the "five ways", take the second left, then travel to the "three ways" and take the first left, then carry on five more miles to the Aboriginal station, where the runway is.' The driver was worried we wouldn't get there before the tide ran out, and insisted on leaving right away.

I was a slow packer, and by the time I'd got back on deck the shuttle boat had just left. I felt a bit empty as I waved goodbye to Joe and the others.

The captain was furious that I'd missed the shuttle. As he was now the radio operator too, he organised a lift for me the next day with one of the small boats that was heading north to Weipa for maintenance. I could catch the plane from there, he said.

Late that afternoon a small plane flew in low over our ship. It was slightly bigger than the one we normally used for spotting prawns, and as it was almost dark it was too late for that anyway.

The captain headed for the radio room, and Tim followed. The news was not good. The shuttle boat had not made it to the station.

Tim was worried. He speculated that if the group got into trouble before reaching the river, the plane would have spotted them or their wreckage. Assuming that they'd made it to the river, the tide would have left them high and dry by now. Tim's best bet was that they'd taken a wrong turn and were now stuck in the mud. If they stayed in the boat they'd be safe from crocodiles and death adders, but mosquitoes would be a problem in that swampy country.

Late the next day the small plane spotted them pushing the shuttle boat along a muddy creek bed. Help was sent from the Aboriginal station on the following high tide, and they were rescued. They reached the station late that evening, covered in mud and mosquito bites. The plane picked them up the next day.

I was glad to hear this news as I boarded the small boat for the overnight journey to Weipa. Phil, the captain of the small boat, offered me a job. It seemed quite a sane boat after the one I was leaving, but I declined, telling him about my mate, Joe. Phil said that if I wanted to I could fly down and get him. Mates were important, he said, and good men were hard to find in the Gulf of Carpentaria. I shook my head and told him, 'I've had enough of prawns.'

I was picked up at Townsville Airport by a rep from the fishing-boat company, taken to their office and paid up. The bursar asked if I had heard about the lost crew and the map the captain had drawn. 'Back to front and the wrong way around,' he said, 'as if they were coming from the station instead of going to it—and not even marking the entrance to the river. The guy must be a nutcase.'

The bursar hadn't seen Joe since he'd been paid up two days before. So, with my swag over my shoulder, I headed for the Commercial Hotel. That was where we'd had our going-away party when the ship had left Townsville.

A few beers later, Joe walked in. We weren't surprised at finding each other so easily. We were just so confident about life, about everything. Joe had taken a quick trip up to Cairns while he was waiting for me.

We had a few more beers and then decided to buy two

bottles of rum, some coke, a carton of beer, an esky and some ice, and move on.

It wasn't long before we were out in the bush again, listening to the ABC radio coverage of the America's Cup yacht race. That was followed by a song that went, 'It's all for me grog, me jolly jolly grog, beer wine and tobacco'.

I don't know how long we drove for that night, or how we ended up talking about getting a boat to Singapore, but it sure was good to pull out that big faded blue tarpaulin.

When we got back to Perth we drew some money out of the bank, took out a money order and sent away by mail for two tickets on a boat to London via Singapore.

But during our few weeks in Perth before departure, Joe got smitten with a girl and decided to stay and get married.

We didn't rekindle our friendship again until many years later. But mates—especially army mates—never forget each other, and our friendship and trust in each other will always be there.

And the big ship was leaving the end of the wharf

The gap between the wharf and the ship increased. Outstretched hands parted company. Streamers hung on until they were swallowed up by the gap. Now wider than you could jump, it would soon be further than you could throw a honky nut: an empty space that has no name but separates family and friends in an anonymous fashion.

Small waves lapped the Plimsoll line. Butterflies were swarming in my empty stomach as I waved goodbye to my sisters. Thoughts of new horizons could not fill the emptiness. The tradition in our family is that you don't stop waving until the car is out of sight or the plane is less than a speck in the sky—or, in this case, until the ship is over the horizon.

I found my cabin. There were six bunks. Only one was taken, so I dropped my sausage bag on the one next to the porthole and introduced myself. Our eyes met in a comfortable way. We shared a brotherly handshake and a look of recognition. He was about my age, but more than that: there was something about him that was familiar. Confident, calm and disturbed came to mind.

Some people talk about character like it's something you find on the supermarket shelf. But the army had developed the character we had come to recognise in each other. It was not the same as it had been before, and it never would be again. When you get out of the army and you can't find the shelf or even the aisle in the supermarket that stocks the kind of character people talk about, you tend to go a little bit quiet and want to get out of that supermarket pretty quick. You know there has to be a change, but there's no one to lead you, and you find it hard to trust people who don't know what you're talking about. So there is comfort when you recognise someone who does.

The bar to adventure

I headed for the ship's bar, which was full of strangers, all travelling north on the open sea. The waves that lapped the Plimsoll line were now ocean swells. The adventure had begun.

The first leg of our one-way journey from Perth to London would take us to Singapore on a Russian ship. The *Khabarovsk* was a small cargo ship that had been converted to carry passengers in 1970 when there was a tremendous increase in world travel. To take advantage of this boom, a lot of old ships and planes were brought back into service and converted to carry passengers.

The drinks were cheap: beer and vodka mostly, nothing fancy. The Russian barmaids did not use cash registers—they used an abacus and a moneybag tied around their waist. They were good-looking people, in a serious sort of way, and did not like jokes.

I sat on a stool and looked at my drink. The longer I looked at it the more it became mine, and the more I drank the closer our relationship became. Even the glass felt familiar.

As time passed, Australia disappeared, and family and friends became only butterflies swimming in my no-longer-so-empty stomach.

I thought about this metaphoric imbalance for some time. Both things seemed to be influenced by drink—Australia disappearing and the butterflies swimming in my stomach. I could understand the butterfly thing, but Australia disappearing was a puzzle.

I raised my head and sat up straighter on my stool. The thought of making new friends gave me hope, and my glass was no longer so important. The character I'd met in my cabin sat down next to me, and we soon became involved in a deep and meaningful discussion about things disappearing. After some time and a few more drinks, our talk drifted to army experiences. We were both ex–National Service veterans trying to find out who we were—or maybe who we would have been if our civilian life had not been so rudely interrupted.

His name was Bob, but he didn't want to be Bob anymore, so right there he changed his name to Randal. He said he planned to grow long hair and a beard, buy a long dark-red leather coat when we got to Singapore and forget (as best he could) that he was ever in the army.

I told Randal the story of the last time I'd visited Singapore.

It was two years ago, in the army, where doing what we were told came naturally—no questions asked. We had a short stopover in Singapore to refuel and change pilots, before heading further north to the war.

The Qantas 707 was packed full of Australian soldiers. We were told that the plane would be on the ground in Singapore for some time without air conditioning, and if we wanted to get off the plane we would have to wear a civilian shirt over our army shirt, because Singapore did not want to be seen as taking sides in the war. Perhaps they hadn't heard about the domino theory. Well, talk about laugh and be insulted at the same time. It was a strange sight, watching one hundred proud and well trained Australian Army soldiers putting civilian shirts on over their uniforms and pretending to be civilians.

Mine was a bright-red-and-yellow Hawaiian floral print. That was the first insult of that war; there would be many more in the years to follow.

Randal was looking forward to the Singapore stopover as a new starting point in life. I, too, was looking for a new outlook on life, but I had no idea where or when the new direction would start.

On arrival, armed immigration police lined us up on the ship's main deck, and any man who had long hair or a beard had his passport confiscated. This included me and Randal. The police said they would return our passports at the airport in four days' time, when we were due to fly out.

At the time, the Singaporean police were known for grabbing long-haired local men off the streets and throwing them in a van, where someone would cut their hair off. The conservative government associated long hair and beards with drugs and hippies, and was trying to clean up Singapore's image.

So we were left standing there, disturbed and annoyed, while the police threw our passports into a chalk ring drawn on the deck as a 'no man's land', for persona non grata. This did not help us to get over our army brainwashing against Asians. I suppose armies always denigrate their enemy, so you don't feel too bad if you have to shoot them.

After some delay we finally got off the ship, found accommodation and explored Singapore. Randal bought his magnificent coat and some grass. I bought a backpack, a portable cassette player and a few Bob Dylan tapes. I was tired of wearing green, so I gave most of my army clothes to a short skinny little fellow who worked in the kitchen where we were staying. He could have used them like a horse blanket they were so big on him, but he was happy to get them all the same. The only clothes I had left now were the ones I was wearing, and my old army jumper. I was fit and strong; a northern hemisphere winter was of no concern to me while I was in warm Singapore.

We flew on to London, our gateway to the world. Randal and I swapped addresses and parted company. It was very cold. I went looking for something warm to wear and, as luck would have it, I found the perfect place and bought a great coat. It was actually called a 'greatcoat'. It cost ten pounds, and it was magnificent feeling so warm when the weather was so cold.

Following a backpackers sign, I found cheap accommodation for the night. It wasn't the most desirable, however, so the next day I went looking for a better place, and eventually moved into a shared house with some people I met at a pub.

Simon was from South Africa. He'd had a similar army experience to mine, and we quickly became friends, exploring London together on foot. He was a calm but disturbed person who couldn't stay in one place long. A few years before, I hadn't known anyone who was disturbed. Or perhaps I just hadn't recognised the look.

After a couple of weeks, Simon moved to Scotland.

Carlsberg

Walking had a calming effect on me. I walked every day for four or five weeks, in all directions, and still didn't see all of London, but I did try just about all of its beers and lagers. Carlsberg was the best, so I bought a sheet of thick plastic for protection from the snow and left England in search of Carlsberg.

My heavy coat and that big sheet of plastic sure came in handy, as it was below freezing when the ferry arrived in Belgium. With my greatcoat and backpack on, I headed down the snowy white road.

The snow held onto the last of the daylight, giving me enough time to organise myself before dark took over. There was about a foot of snow along the sides of the autobahn and I made camp in the woods next to it, wrapping myself and my backpack in the plastic sheet and leaving my boots on, of course. I listened to some music, and opened a tin of stew and a bottle of beer.

I never did see a sign to Carlsberg. I just turned south instinctively, to where the weather should get warmer: simple logic. Little did I realise that Carlsberg was the name of a brewery on the outskirts of Copenhagen, and that if I wanted to get there I should have turned left when I got off the ferry and travelled north towards the cold.

The snow continued to fall, and gave me protection from

the wind as it covered my plastic sheet. I was warm, and as long as I could get fresh air I was going to be all right. I had my tin of stew and just the one bottle of beer, for I wasn't about to have to answer the call of nature during the middle of the night.

One afternoon, near a town called Aalist, I was caught in a blizzard. Common sense told me that I needed to find warm shelter, so when I saw the lights of a village I crossed a snowy field and went to the town bar.

No one in the bar spoke English, but I managed to buy a beer. There was a picture of Australia on my wallet; the barman saw it and smiled. Shortly after that, a guy who all the other patrons knew came in, shaking hands all round. He was a local motorbike hero who had been to Australia. He could speak a little English, and proceeded to tell me that ten years ago two famous Australian tennis players had visited when their car had broken down on the autobahn.

By the time I'd finished my beer the bar was packed with people saying 'Austraalee' and patting me on the back. I don't know who the two tennis players were, but they sure did leave a good impression. With that, I was given food and lodging for the night, albeit in the back of a minivan. I was warm and dry, and if that minivan had been four feet longer I would have been comfortable, too.

Munich

Without even realising it, I was on my way to Munich, famous for its beer and beer festivals. I hiked through the snow and, cold but happy and content, camped outside almost every night until I made it to Munich, arriving just before the 1972 Olympic Games to plenty of work and good beer.

I bumped into Randal at the famous Hofbrauhaus beer hall. He was passing through on his way to Greece. I decided to stay in Germany, get a flat and settle down for a while.

Munich was a whole new world to me. It seemed like everyone was either stoned or rolling a joint. Finding work was easy, but accommodation was expensive, so I took temporary shelter in one of the newly finished athletes quarters, which had central heating, a bed, a TV, a fridge—everything. There was even a key in the door. No one seemed to mind, and I only had to step over a small fence to get in. There was no security or police. What a great place, I thought.

As the Games got closer, I introduced myself to some of the athletes. I didn't pretend to be an athlete—they just assumed I was one. I made it quite clear that I was just there for the beer, which got a few laughs, but eventually I realised I would have to move on, so with a couple of new friends I'd met at the Hofbrauhaus I rented a flat on the shady side of town where not many tourists go. Beer, food and lodging were much, much cheaper there, and the tram made access to the city easy.

A short walk down Marienplatz and there was our beer hall.

The Hofbrauhaus was an incredible meeting place; most nights there would have been several hundred people singing, drinking, dancing and having a good time. Most were tourists in town only for a few days. We didn't consider ourselves tourists, as we had a permanently reserved table that we used every night; on weekends we used it both afternoons and nights. We could seat about fifteen at our long heavy old-fashioned wooden table with bench seating on each side. One end was left open so that Maria, who could carry ten beer steins at one time without spilling a drop, could slide the steins to the people at the far end. There were many rows of these tables, and we were proud to have our own.

Owned by the German state of Bavaria, the Hofbrauhaus was a place where prisoners could work off their parole time. Maria and her partner, who we called Barf the Bouncer, were part of a staff of about twenty. They lived upstairs and were a bit rough, but not really dangerous. We became friends in a foreign sort of way.

I had an understanding with Barf that if I was standing on a table 'for viewing purposes' when there was a fight in the beer hall, and he slammed his baton down on the table, I would get down immediately. As I was a large, conspicuous person, this allowed him to show some authority. As my reward I was treated fairly at the bar with a full stein of beer, not half froth like the tourists got.

Off like a piece of cheese

One chilly day, I was warmed not by the fire in the beer hall but by a gorgeous girl from Kentucky who had lost her sunglasses and a pair of kid gloves that had belonged to her mother. We literally bumped into each other as she emerged from the revolving door of the Hofbrauhaus. This was followed by an awkward exchange of words, in German and in English: 'Sorry', 'Entschuldigung', 'Are you okay?' But as I reached for my translation book the language barrier disappeared with a friendly smile, the warmth of which has never been exceeded.

We sat down at 'our' table and shared a beer. Communication was difficult at first, as one of us had a foreign accent, but a friendship soon developed that surpassed any superficial obstacles.

I was happy to help Mary Ann look for her sunglasses and gloves, but Wolfgang from behind the food counter, which doubled as the lost-and-found, wasn't all that friendly, I didn't know how to say 'sunglasses' or 'gloves' in German, and trying to explain with sign language didn't seem to help. Wolfgang could speak broken English when it suited him, but on this occasion his arrogant smile made it clear that he was not going to be helpful. Ignoring his smile, I looked at the food on offer and suggested to Mary Ann that we get something to eat.

My new friend seemed a bit more sophisticated than I was, so I ordered a platter of cheese and crackers. When Maria delivered the food, it was easy to tell that the cheese was off: it was soft and runny and smelt like an old shoe, so I took it back to the food counter.

I only knew a few words in German, but I proceeded to explain to Wolfgang that the cheese was off.

Wolfgang said, 'Is good. Camembert.'

I said, 'I don't care who made it, mate, it's bad.'

He kept saying, 'Is good, is good. Camembert.'

This argument went on for some time, until Wolfgang threw the cheese on the floor and jumped up and down on it. He was obviously quite upset, and in the process taught me a few more words in German.

My friends and I had been working at one of Munich's oldest, most exclusive hotels, the Vier Jahreszeiten (Four Seasons) on Maximilianstrasse. One of its wings was being renovated by an overtly gay Texan, and our job was to move furniture around and take down paintings and rehang them in almost the same spot.

All the rooms in the renovated wing had big bathtubs, large white towels and robes, shampoo and bubble bath, and after work I sometimes took a bath. When I told Mary Ann that the tubs were deep and wide and six foot long, her eyes lit up. She described the awful showers in the shared bathrooms at the youth hostel, and the woman there who yelled 'Schnell! Schnell!' ('Hurry up! Hurry up!') if you took more than two minutes.

As the hotel was just around the corner, and I had a key to the staff elevator, I asked Mary Ann if she was interested in a luxurious white tiled bathroom all to herself.

The next day when we got there it was late in the afternoon.

Just as we arrived, two limousines pulled up. Willy Brandt, the previous year's Nobel Peace Prize winner and current chancellor of Germany, got out. He went inside with a few security people in black suits. The hotel day staff had left, and no one questioned us as we got into the staff elevator.

The new wing was not completely ready for use, and we were the only people there. I ran a bubble bath for Mary Ann and then kept lookout, sitting in a bay window in the hallway. The warm April sun was setting over Munich.

We spent the next few days getting to know each other and touring the art galleries and the science and industry museum. When the skies were sunny, a group of my friends often played non-contact grid-iron football at the Englischer Garten (English Garden), using a frisbee instead of a football. Mary Ann and her friend and travelling companion, Kitty, would join us.

When Mary Ann went home to America I was a little lost. I had her address in Kentucky and an invitation, and was challenged by the idea that there was more to life than just going to pubs and beer festivals. My Munich friends were good friends, but without much direction. We were all just having a good time in a foreign country. Sometimes you don't know something's missing until you find it.

As I looked around the Hofbrauhaus on my last night—with its china statues, my friends, the tourists and the trombone-and-piano-accordion band that almost continually played oom pah pah music—I knew I had to leave Germany and explore new horizons.

My cheeks were flushed, my ears were warm, my direction was unknown but clear: I was going to follow my heart.

This challenge, although not easy, felt natural and compelling. I had a good last night with my beer hall friends; it was one of those emotional times when you know you need to say goodbye and move on.

England

The next day I packed my backpack, waved goodbye to my friends and headed north to Rotterdam, where I hoped to get a working passage on a cargo ship to the USA.

I was in Rotterdam for four days, staying at the Blue Peter, the Mission to Seafarers refuge. (In the days of old sailing ships, harbour towns all over the world had a refuge for sailors called a Blue Peter. It was a place to get cheap food and charitable hospitality, as well as a place where you could sign on for a new ship.)

I tried all the ships in port, but had no luck. I was frustrated at not finding a ship straight away. The slight language barrier did not help. Not deterred, I decided to head back to England to work things out from there.

The return journey across the English Channel was quite a different trip. I was the only passenger, and I was a different person: vulnerable and no longer emotionally self-contained. I stood on the open deck with butterflies in my stomach. The night was dark and lonely. It was freezing cold, and I felt it. The sea was rough, and my greatcoat did not protect me as it had previously in similar conditions. Emotional longing was new to me. I was excited, and the emptiness was lost in the cold of the night.

London, Earls Court Tavern. Looking out of the bar window I saw a sign on the pavement advertising cheap flights to the USA with Lloyds International.

'I wonder how cheap?' I said to the barman.

'Ask that guy at the other end of the bar. He works for them.'

Carl, the guy at the other end of the bar, told me the price, what I needed to do, and where to get a visa for the USA. We had a few drinks together. He was knowledgeable about Australia, and even recognised my Australian GP army boots. They were the envy of the other armies—especially the Yanks, who would pay anything for Australian boots.

'Did you go to Vietnam?' Carl asked.

'Yes, I was conscripted.'

'You mean you were forced to go?'

'I was conscripted into the army. During recruit training one day I was told to fall out from the parade and report to the dentist. While I was gone, the rest of the parade were asked by one of the corporals if they had any objections to going to Vietnam. If so, they could give their reason, in private, when they were marched in to the Platoon Officer. Apparently the officer was doing a survey of some kind. After the dentist, I joined the end of the parade as the remaining recruits were being marched into the officer's hut. When my turn came, with a corporal front and back screaming "Left! Right! Left! Right!", I marched in and saluted the officer. He said, "What's your answer?" I didn't know what he was talking about, and felt under pressure. The officer looked up, and said loudly, "Recruit, what is your answer?" So I said, "*Four, Sir!*"

Carl liked that story, and we chatted comfortably for some time. The next day I met him in his office—the front room of an old terrace house in Earls Court—and bought a ticket to Bangor, Maine, in the USA. It would still be a fair way to Kentucky, but at least I'd be in the right country.

My first visit to the US embassy in London to get a tourist visa failed. The embassy man said I needed to prove that I had enough money to support myself for the duration of my stay in the USA. If I could do that, then he might consider giving me a short-term visa.

After a call to my sister Trish in Perth and the cabling of money, I returned to the embassy. The embassy man advised me that he still thought I might be an illegal immigrant risk, even though, 'much to his surprise', I satisfied their financial requirements. This official behind the glass window didn't seem to like me; perhaps it was the long hair and the beard or the peace sign I wore around my neck. There was a war on, and I guess I fitted the description of a hippie anti-war protester. I wasn't sure what I was, other than someone wondering if 'four' was not the wrong answer.

The second refusal didn't alter my intentions one little bit, although getting to the States was now going to require a little more effort. Flying to Toronto in Canada seemed the only choice—I'd then jump the border into the USA and hitchhike south to Cincinnati, then cross the Ohio River to Kentucky. This would take a little longer, but it didn't matter. My direction was clear.

Carl was happy to change my ticket to Toronto, but when I returned to confirm my flight two days before departure he informed me that there had been a slight change in the flight plan because of some mistake about Lloyds not paying landing fees in Toronto. We would now be landing in Bangor after all, and Lloyds would provide a bus for those who wanted to go on to Toronto. The bottom line was that I would need a transit visa for the USA.

The man at the American Embassy put on an insincere smile when he saw me coming. Having had my tourist visa application refused twice already, I suspected there could be a problem with the transit visa.

'So, don't you want to go to Cincinnati anymore?' he said.

'Yes, I do. I really do.' And I explained the reason.

'A girl! Ah,' he said, and looked again at my passport, turning the pages slowly. 'How come it's stamped "Not valid for North Vietnam"?'

I told him it was because Australia was at war with North Vietnam, the same as America.

'Is that right?' he said. 'And did you serve there?'

'Yes,' I said. He seemed satisfied and, after a few more questions from him and promises from me, he stamped my passport with a B2 non-immigrant visa stamp for six months.

I had been fooled by the name Lloyds International. It sounded important, but it was a small independent airline company; in fact, it couldn't have been smaller. The plane was old and it broke down in Iceland, causing us to spend the night in the airport terminal. Outside it was cold and cloudy. Inside it was warm and the bar was open.

Touchdown USA

The plane arrived in Bangor late the next evening. Buses for Toronto awaited the other passengers. Carl—who was not only Lloyds' office worker but also its chief steward and baggage handler—asked how I intended to get to Cincinnati. I told him I thought I'd wait till morning and hitch a ride south, but that I wasn't looking forward to spending another night in an airport.

'Why don't you fly on with us to the west coast?' Carl said. 'It won't cost you anything—we have some cancelled tickets. You'll be fed and have somewhere to sleep. You can spend tomorrow afternoon sightseeing in Seattle, then fly back with us the next morning.'

It was dark and wet outside, so I said okay. In the next thirty hours I flew across the USA twice.

Arriving back in Bangor late the next evening after more maintenance problems, I found myself in the same situation. Carl, who was trying to be nice, told me to wait at the bottom of the steps, on the tarmac. I waited there and, after all the other passengers had gone inside the terminal, Carl came down and asked if I would like to hitch a flight from the domestic terminal to Cincinnati.

'Sure,' I said. So he walked into the hangar, drove back out in a pick-up truck and told me to jump on the back.

We drove under the belly of the aircraft. He gave me an

odd-looking key in the shape of a wool bale hook, and pointed to the luggage door. I stood up on the truck and undid the locks, and the door lowered. I climbed into the belly of the 707, found a light switch, found my backpack, then climbed out and closed the luggage door behind me, being sure, of course, to lock it properly.

We drove down the mile-long runway. Carl told me that it was designed to carry B52 bombers, just in case America decided to bomb Russia.

Carl was a man who would go out of his way to help people. At first I'd thought it was all just an act—part of his job—but he was the same whether he was behind the ticket counter or serving meals on the plane. He always did his best to make you smile. The fact that he was gay served as an education to me; it broke down the stereotypes I'd grown up with. I enjoyed his company.

I'd been taught prejudice in the army, and before that when I'd worked in small mining towns—which sounds very similar to 'small-minded towns'—and before when I was growing up in the conservative 'don't rock the boat' city of Perth.

Getting over prejudices of all sorts was a relief, and one of the reasons I was travelling the world. I felt safe with Carl, driving along that B52 runway in the middle of the night, smoking cigarettes and talking about the Olympic Games in Munich.

On reaching the small plane terminal, Carl introduced me to the waiting airport manager. He mentioned that I had *also* served in Vietnam. I wondered who the other *also* was, but before I could say a word Carl shook my hand, wished me good luck, gave the manager a hug and was gone.

Bob, the manager, had lost a son in the army. He was a big man who looked like he hadn't smiled in a long time. Carl had told him of my plans, and he told me I could sleep in the flight briefing room until I could hitch a flight south. There was coffee and biscuits (which they called cookies), cool drinks and a big leather sofa to sleep on.

Bob said they were sending a small plane down to Boston, Massachusetts, to pick up Sandy Koufax, a famous baseball pitcher, coach and broadcaster, and that I could get a lift. I looked at the big map on the wall and saw that Boston was closer to Cincinnati than Bangor was.

The lift was okay with the pilot, but the weather closed in at the last minute and single-engine planes weren't allowed to take off, so it was back to the flight briefing room, leather sofa and cookies for me.

I was embarrassed when the night flight crews from some of the larger domestic aircraft started tiptoeing in, saying 'Don't wake up the Aussie' as they prepared for their flights.

On the road again

The next day was cold but sunny. I decided to leave the airport and try the more traditional way of hitching a lift. The fresh air and open space of the freeway made a nice change, but it didn't last long.

The first car that stopped was a highway patrol car. It pulled up behind me with a brief siren sound and lights flashing. The patrolman got out and gestured with his finger that I was in the wrong place, and that where he was standing—next to his patrol car—was the right place.

Rather than argue about something so trivial, I walked over to the patrol car.

'How're you doing?' I said.

Well, one thing led to another, and after a brief exchange he said, 'I'm afraid I'm going to have to arrest you.' I noticed that he had two pearl-handled guns and wore them low, like a cowboy.

'Why?' I asked.

'It's against the law to hitchhike in Maine,' he said, and asked to see some identification. I gave him my passport.

'We don't get many hippies around here. Where you going to, with your long hair and dressed like that? I hope for your sake you're not carrying any drugs.'

'No, Sir,' I said. He walked around to the back of the patrol car and told me to put my backpack in the 'trunk'.

'I'm not going to cuff you, and you can even sit in the front seat, but I warn you, I'm a crack shot with my forty-fives.' I didn't say a word, but I sure was worried.

When we got to the police station he sat me down in the waiting room and disappeared behind closed doors. The outside doors were not locked, and I could see the patrol car that had my backpack in the trunk. There was no one around but me. I pondered the possibilities of my situation, but waited until the highway patrolman came back out. His neck seemed redder than I'd noticed before, like he had been up against a heater. He said, 'We're going for a ride to the lock-up. You can sit in the front if you like.

'A good patrolman is like a good hound dog: he keeps his nose close to the ground,' he told me on the way to the lock-up. Then he pulled into a twenty-four-hour highway restaurant and said, 'Let's get something to eat.'

After we'd sat down in the restaurant he said, 'You're not under arrest. The chief said I shouldn't have arrested you and told me to take you out to lunch.'

'I'll have the steak, thanks,' I said, and smiled with relief. We talked easily through lunch. I asked if it was all right to hitchhike on aeroplanes; he said that had nothing to do with him.

I thanked the officer for lunch and he gave me a ride back to the airport. We even swapped addresses.

Back at the airport, Bob called me into the briefing room and introduced me to three light-aircraft pilots who were heading down to New York to learn how to load the new Jumbo 747s. They decided the best time to land at Kennedy Airport would be early in the morning when it wouldn't be too busy.

We took off for New York very early the next morning in a small six-seater. Our approach to Kennedy Airport seemed incredibly busy to me. As we neared New York the air traffic controller on the radio said, 'Now, you boys, don't worry, but there's an Air Italia DC8 passing right over you and you might feel a little turbulence.'

As the big jet flew over us I gained new respect for Italians and all the other people who were responsible for my safety.

'Kennedy approach, this is November 6745 Bravo, 5000 feet, estimate Kennedy 21.'

'November 6745 Bravo, Kennedy approach, you are clear for visual approach runway 11 left, call Kennedy tower 118.1 at 5 miles.'

'Kennedy tower, this is November 6745 Bravo, 5 mile final. Runway 11 left.'

'November 6745 Bravo, clear to land, call Kennedy ground 123.9 clear of the active.'

Then as soon as our wheels touched the tarmac, ground control came onto the radio, saying, 'Now, you boys, don't hang around on the runway too long, there's a big Italian right up your ass.'

I thanked my new friends for the lift, and in the first light of day I wandered the tarmac looking at the planes.

The new Jumbo 747 was bigger than you could point a stick at. No one asked me who I was or what I was doing on the tarmac. I started to think I must look important, walking around in army greens and boots and carrying a backpack, but when I went inside the passenger terminal the door locked behind me and suddenly I was with all these ordinary people.

It was so crowded I just wanted to get out of there.

I paid for a Delta Airlines ticket to Cincinnati. Then I found a soundproof phone box with no visible phone—just a dial and a place to put your money. When you haven't got a mouthpiece to talk into or an earpiece to listen to, and you're just standing there with your hands in your pockets making a phone call to someone you've been thinking a lot about for a couple of weeks, when she says 'Hello', you don't know which way to turn.

I had spoken to Mary Ann's parents from Seattle and Bangor, but this was the first time I had spoken to Mary Ann since Munich. Her voice was soft and warm. A few hours later I was in her arms. The next part of my life was just beginning.

My first trip to the USA lasted six months, until I was called back to Australia for the weddings of my sisters Trish and Sue. Mary Ann followed seven months later, when she'd finished her master's degree. We briefly settled in Perth, but the culture shock was too great, so we moved to the more multicultural city of Melbourne for several years, and then on to Pittwater in New South Wales for a year.

Bosun the black Labrador

Every morning his ears pricked up as I rowed across the bay—or so the woman who owned him said. He had either extremely good hearing or a sixth sense, because his timing was impeccable.

I would row our small dinghy across from Scotland Island to Church Point on the mainland every morning, where I would start my day as the local ferry operator.

I know Scotland Island sounds like two countries, but it's simply a small island on Pittwater, an inland waterway north of Sydney. To be more precise, it's the only island on Pittwater. Back then in 1977 it had a population of almost one hundred people. It has no vehicles or roads, so everything travels on the water. It looks a picture, and I am happy to say we started our married life there.

Our house was on Scotland Island, but the community centre was a small park on the mainland next to the Church Point jetty, where there was a small general store, a grog shop and a marina. Bosun lived on the hill behind Church Point.

From Scotland Island to Church Point was five hundred metres or so across the bay. The trip only took ten minutes once I started rowing, but getting the dinghy adrift from the muddy shore while trying not to stand on too many soldier crabs if the tide was low was an effort. Pushing the dinghy across twenty metres of mudflats also took time, and sometimes a few swear words.

Bosun, up at his place on the hill behind Church Point, must have been about half a mile from those mudflats where I anchored the dinghy. I describe all this just so you can understand what a clever dog he was.

After I rowed across to Church Point, I tied the dinghy up to the jetty from the bow, and then threw a stern line to the bollard at the jetty park. I walked around to fasten it, then climbed onto the ferry, checked the oil and water, started the engine, checked the pumps, let go the securing ropes and then set the engine to slow ahead. This all took about twenty minutes.

Bosun timed it down to the last second, and somewhere between my rowing across the bay and tying up the dinghy, he made his move. The woman who owned him said it was always the same, every morning: Bosun would jump to his feet like he was startled, then run flat-out down the hill to the jetty.

The ferry would just be moving away from the jetty as Bosun pounded down the road then along the jetty and made a last-second leap to catch the ferry. Sometimes the ferry would be a good few feet from the jetty, but Bosun would always make it.

Except for one time. I don't know what happened that day, but he missed his jump and landed in the ocean. I kept going, and he followed, so eventually I turned back and picked him up. Then, to top it all off, when we got to Scotland Island to pick up a passenger, Bosun, for the first time ever, jumped ashore and took off up the hill and didn't stop until he got to the water tank.

The water tank was the only freshwater source on the

island. It was fed by a pipe that ran under the bay from the mainland. It was supposed to be only for fire emergencies, but the school kids used the tap for a drink, and animals drank out of the bowl underneath that caught the drips, so nothing was wasted.

The houses on Scotland Island were supposed to manage their own water supply through rainwater tanks, but if the water tank was higher up the hill than your house, then siphoning the water into your rainwater tank became tempting. During a drought, community cooperation was essential. The first house down the road from the tank would start siphoning; this would normally take about three days. Then the house down from that one would join their garden hose to the first one's. Our house was the tenth in line, which was a lot of hoses—about ten, I believe. I was soon to learn how important water was.

Anyway Bosun was up there having a drink, so I thought he'd be all right and would probably catch the ferry back on my next trip to the island. But later that day Mary Ann, who was pregnant at the time, sent word that her waters had broken, so I assumed a bit of urgency and forgot all about Bosun.

I rushed home, and our first son was born later that day at Mona Vale hospital.

A few days later, Bev, the woman who ran the ferry company, said she hoped we had plenty of water. I didn't know what she was talking about. Although I'd heard the same thing on some of those old movies—'lots of hot water'—I never had understood what that was all about. I soon learned, however, why we would need lots of water. Nappies—two-foot square bits of white cloth—required lots of washing water, even with a twin-tub washing machine.

The next morning as I pulled away from the Church Point jetty, there was no sign of my old friend. I went to visit him that lunchtime at his place: it seemed he had just lost interest.

It's a strange feeling when a dog looks at you and you know he knows something you don't.

The park, the artist and the sheriff

Life for Mary Ann and me got pretty busy then, what with a new baby son and the ferry wars heating up.

The basic idea with the ferry was to pick up as many paying passengers as you could, all the while trying to make it as hard as possible for the rival ferry company to operate. At times there was a bit of danger. It was all to do with the rules of the sea: you could do anything as long as it was legal.

In between the last few runs at night, both of us ferry drivers would share a few beers in the park next to the jetty. There was a grog shop next to the park, where some of the passengers also bought beer to bring over to the island; it was the community's get-together place, where you could talk to your neighbours.

One night Jim, the outboard motor repairman who had a small shed in one corner of the park, enquired about Bosun. When I told him the story, he said the DJ from 2JJ reckoned when a new baby enters the scene sometimes a dog feels rejected.

Apart from drinking in this little park, we also gambled. The idea was that when you finished your beer you threw your empty can into the rubbish bin about twenty feet away. It cost twenty cents a go. It wasn't that easy, especially if there was a wind. Depending on how many people played, of course, there could be a few dollars in the kitty. The local policeman joined in. He was a quiet sort of a person—seemed a nice guy, somebody you could probably trust. He always left his hat in the car; this made everyone feel a bit more relaxed because, strictly speaking, our little game was illegal.

I never knew that Australia had sheriffs until one night a locally well-known artist asked me if, on short notice, I would do a late-night ferry run. He said he had heard through the grapevine that his ex-wife and her big Maori boyfriend planned on stealing some of his paintings.

'If they do come up here,' he said, 'I might need to pack up and leave quickly. It's only the paintings I'm worried about. I'll pay you well.'

Sure enough, two nights later the late-night call came, and to the rescue I went. Some of the paintings were so big they wouldn't fit in the ferry. I asked him if he'd like me to call the water police.

'Shit, no!' he said.

What an odd response, I thought.

It made more sense the next morning. I'd just finished the school run when standing on the jetty I saw this big man in civilian clothes with a star-shaped badge like a sheriff's.

I tied up. He jumped on board and said, 'Howdy. Did you pick up a passenger and paintings from Taylors Bay last night?'

'Who are you?' I said.

'I'm Sheriff Peterson. I'm the Sheriff from theMagistrates Court.'

'No, you're not. We don't have sheriffs.'

'Yes, we do; we're the people who serve summonses, and in this case I have a summons for your late-night passenger.'

'What did he do?'

'Fraud. He buys expensive prints and paints them to look like they're original. Then he rents an upmarket house like the one over there in Taylors Bay, advertises a sale of original artwork, makes a pile of money, then buggers off as soon as someone gets suspicious.'

'You don't look like a sheriff.'

'I get that all the time, and quite frankly I'm sick of it. Do you want to see my gun or something?'

'It's just a bit strange to hassle a bloke for painting over a print and then selling it. I mean, if he buys the print fair and square and improves it with a bit of paint, well, good luck to him—he's not hurting anyone.'

'Yes, he is. What about the artist who paints for a living? This guy is using his prints and his name without his permission.'

After the school run, the next run was the mail delivery—a peaceful time in the morning to reflect on the day. Bev sometimes hopped on board and helped sort the mail.

'That guy really is a sheriff,' she said that morning, 'so be a bit careful. We don't need any trouble, especially after you nearly forced that other ferry onto the beach yesterday afternoon.'

'That was nothing,' I said, 'and anyhow, it was completely legal—he would have done the same thing to me. He tried to overtake me illegally. If I'd let him get away with that, especially on the school run, then the kids would all want to travel with him and we'd lose a lot of business.'

After the mail run I took the sheriff over to Taylors Bay, where he checked out our departed artist's rented house—a waterfront home on the most beautiful bay in the national park.

That's about all I can remember about our time on

Scotland Island, except for a few storms and the odd bushfire. Oh, and taking the end-of-year football team away up the Hawkesbury River—that was something to remember.

The thing I miss most, though, is Bosun, the black Labrador.

Good ol' boys

Henry Ford was a little different. He was from Tennessee. He'd lied about his age and joined the navy at sixteen. He was well travelled and had had many experiences. He was on the *West Virginia* when it went down in Pearl Harbor. He still remembers the screams of the other boys in the burning oil.

I spent two years in Somerset, Kentucky, with my wife Mary Ann and our first son, Colby. He was only a few months old when we arrived in Polaski County. His grandpa and grandma and Mary Ann's seven brothers and sisters lived three hours north, on the Kentucky side of Cincinnati.

We had a nice A-frame house on Lake Cumberland. A deer track passed through the steep descent to the lake. I saw it being used only once. Dramatic, it was. Light wet snow was falling on a miserable night, windy, but just light enough to see the lake a hundred yards away. I stepped out onto the freezing balcony, as Australians do in a freezing country.

Wild, it was, like on the bow of a small fishing boat in rough weather. First I heard the family of deer pounding along the track. Then I could see the head of the family, steam coming from his nostrils, turning toward me like an angry skipper in a storm. In a matter of seconds they were gone.

At first I worked for Varna Holt at Americool. A year later I defected to his opposition—Arnold's Cumberland Refrigeration.

A packet of fifty .22 calibre bullets cost eighty cents back then. Most of the good ol' boys carried more powerful weapons, and when they murdered a deer they would strap it to the front of their pick-up truck for everyone to see.

I don't know why they did this, but sometimes it would stay tied to the front of their pick-up for days. If a soldier did this in combat, only a savage would follow him. Its blood dripping down the bonnet, the deer was not for eating but for showing off.

People would walk over to the murdered deer. Fathers would prod it with a finger and their sons would prod it with a stick. Old grocery men would put a foot on the bumper bar, chew a plug of Red Man tobacco and spit out the juice, saying, 'You got a good one there, all right.' These were the good ol' boys: the 'rednecks'.

Henry Ford was different. He'd seen enough killing in World War II. Me, I'd seen enough killing somewhere else. I guess that's why we got on—plus, we both liked a drink.

I often worked with Henry. We travelled all over Kentucky and most of the surrounding states. Without his help I never would have become a journeyman refrigeration mechanic or been able to buy beer. It was illegal to buy beer in Polaski County; in fact, the nearest liquor outlet was in Richmond, about ninety miles away.

We were in Confederate territory, south of the Mason–Dixon line, and not about to pay no Yankee federal tax on beer and 'such'.

This was a dry county and had been for seventy years; some say even longer. You could buy the local moonshine, though—

or 'sky', as it was known—if you knew the right people. We had a few good hiding places in the van in case we were stopped by the county police looking for illegal beer entering the county. If they found any it was normally confiscated, but if you were a tourist there would, of course, be a fine as well.

Henry got caught one night driving while drunk, or DUI (driving under the influence)—'way over the limit', the state trooper from Monticello said. Henry argued and was treated roughly, with bruises to prove it.

Our workshop was in Somerset, the main town in Polaski County. Our office was there too, and a showroom, and Pat, who answered the phone in between knitting penis warmers and being the angel of sanity in that small-minded town.

The Baptist church, its preachers and deacons, they ran that county in all departments—police, education, fire—all of it. Henry wasn't a churchgoer but he worked for a few, who all liked him—especially the bit about Pearl Harbor.

They sure did come to his defence on court day—so many good character references. Varna told the story about Pearl Harbor, and just then one of the good ol' boys on the jury winked at Henry and Henry relaxed a little. Then Arnold, our boss, told a story 'that he believed to be the truth' about how breathing in refrigeration gas can have the same effect as beer on 'those Yankee breathalyser machines'. 'Why, Henry has never stolen anything in his life, and he is a very hard worker,' he added. Then Henry got a second wink from that juror, and he knew he was all right.

That state trooper was real put out by the verdict.

We never did drink beer again while driving past that place where Henry had got pulled over. We were an exception to the rule, since we didn't go to church and we liked a drink.

We made sure we didn't rock the boat, though. We knew our place. We worked hard, we were veterans of foreign wars, we were white, and we never said anything bad about the church.

Red Neck Thinking

We were living among the descendants of some of America's 'First Families'. These were runaway indentured white servants who had come to the hills to hide from the authorities. Like their ancestors, the people we lived among lived simple, isolated lives, raising pigs and growing beans, tomatoes and corn, with some distilling their own 'sky'. Survival was their main concern; education wasn't seen as important. The Bible was their only book. It said what was right and what was wrong. It was the code they lived by—according to the interpretation of their preacher or deacon. It was interesting how those preachers and deacons ended up with the best land, and scorned education.

Arnold was known to have affairs. I asked him once about the adultery clause in the Bible, and he assured me that it was a mistake. 'Anything that good can't be a sin,' he explained. Another explanation I heard more than once about the adultery clause was: 'What if my wife went and got herself paralysed, or suddenly died or something—where would I be then? The Bible didn't take that into consideration, did it? There I'd be, all sad and mourning at the cemetery. Everyone would go home and eat dinner with their wife and I'd be all alone. I don't think God would want that. And anyway, I'm still free, white and over twenty-one, and there's no sign yet of me being an outcast of society.'

It was a pretty tough two years. I was earning $125 a week (overtime was compulsory, but not paid), doing country work, sleeping in a truck cabin with three good ol' boys on a snow-piled road. No one complained—except me, to Mary Ann. I was always glad to get home to Mary Ann and Colby. We lived in the country on a lake, with no close neighbours. Inside our perimeter, normal is what we were. Going to work was a bit like going overseas.

Varna's whistle

There's a strange balance in life that I've been trying to understand. Some people extrapolate on tangents, while others never leave the narrow road their parents walked. The people who killed those deer with high-powered rifles and tied them to the bonnets of their pick-up trucks were simple people guarding their traditions, protecting their values. They were loyal red-blooded good ol' boys with nowhere to go. Pork chops, corn bread, beans, apple pie and coffee.

Varna was one such person. He was a salesman, and the big boss at Americool. He'd had some sort of operation involving a plastic tube. He didn't say what the problem was, but when he farted he whistled. No one said a thing, unless they'd had too much 'sky' and were behind the toolshed. Normally what they said wasn't funny at all, but boy, did we laugh. There wasn't much to laugh about in that environment, but there sure was a need to.

Varna could be as cruel as right and wrong would let him. The only emotion I saw in him was when he used the power he had to sack people—or threaten them with the sack. Looking like a Southern plantation owner or a Kentucky colonel, with a confident expression and a strong stance he would say, 'You can go to the house.'

I saw him sack several people. It was scary. 'You can go to the house,' he'd say, and whoever he said it to was completely at his mercy. 'Yes, Sir, Boss. Whatever you say, Mr Varna, Sir. I'll be good, Boss. Please let me work.' After this was over, Varna felt relieved, like he was just done eatin' a big slice of watermelon. 'Hah, you don't have to go to the house,' he'd say, 'but next time you make sure you turn the light off in the commode, you hear?' Varna took pride in the expressions of a hundred years ago.

'Healing'

Bill Vires Jr worked with us at Americool. He was eighteen years old, his wife was seventeen and their baby son was two. The baby's grandmother was thirty-two and the great-grandmother was forty-seven. The great-great-grandmother wasn't mentioned at all. I was told, 'We don't talk about her.'

When I first met Bill, he invited me to go 'healing'. So 'we-all'—as they say in those parts—drove out to his folks' shack, which was surrounded by car wrecks and healthy stands of corn. It had a pot-belly stove in the middle, which was surrounded by beds, a TV and a fridge, all on a dirt floor. The walls were lined with Ball jars of preserved beans and tomatoes.

Bill introduced 'us'ns' to his family, then took me out the back, saying we were going healing. I didn't know where we were going or what we were going to do. Should I have brought a first aid kit, a paddle or a shotgun? We walked over several hills and saw a few animals and birds and a wild beehive being attacked by a bumblebee, which Bill called a Russian bee. We then went back to the shack, where Mary Ann was having a cup of tea and Bill's family was making a fuss over Colby. We'd only been gone about an hour. Mary Ann and Colby seemed content, and Bill hoped I had enjoyed healing.

Bill's dad, Bill Sr, was seventy-two years old. He showed me his gun and a very old rifle: the one he'd stopped the coal truck with.

'They think they own the road,' he said. 'I told him if he ever comes down this road again, tootin' and swervin' all over the place, I'll blow his goddam head off.'

Mrs Vires stood up and said, 'You can blow his dang head off, but I don't care to hear you cursin' no more.'

Their neighbour Virgil, from three stands of corn up the road, did blow a boy's head off one year. Bill Sr told the story.

It was summer, hot and dusty on the gravel road. 'That dust sure can ruin a fine stand of corn,' Bill Sr said. Anyway, this boy was tearing up and down the road in an old Chevrolet that belonged to some 'no account' from that trailer park down yonder. Virgil went out and told the boy to stop, on account of the dust. The boy took no notice, like a disrespectful city boy, so Virgil went inside and got his gun and waited by the front fence near the gravel road. The next time the boy went past, Virgil blew his head off.

Murder is a federal offence under state police jurisdiction in the US, but on this day the county police came out. An ambulance took the body away and the sheriff interviewed Virgil. No arrest was made; it was considered 'death by misadventure'.

On leaving, the sheriff said, 'Well, Virgil, you did warn him.'

The Doughboy

On the way home from the Vires' house we detoured through Monticello, as the locals do, to buy some of the coleslaw that Ronald makes at the Burger Queen. It's 'sompin' else'.

Ronald, a big soft-spoken friendly man, was also the mayor of Monticello. He loved Australians; he even asked me if I wanted to become a Kentucky colonel. When you bought a burger at his restaurant, Ronald would normally sit down with you for a few minutes and tell you a story. Like this one.

Ronald was at a well-attended town meeting that was being held to decide whether to shift the Doughboy or not. The Doughboy was a brass statue of a World War I soldier that had been erected in the middle of the main street. Back when it was erected there wasn't much traffic, but more recently it had become a problem, some said. Others said we should have more respect for people who fought for the country. It was a 'purty' lively debate, and Ronald got up and spoke. 'Some of my friends want the Doughboy to be moved,' he said, 'and some of my friends want the Doughboy to stay. Let me just say, I am with my friends one hundred per cent.'

The Doltons

There are some funny people in Southern Kentucky. They are comfortably warm and friendly in their own environment, and don't ask or expect too much of other people. But being an outsider, I knew my place.

It's interesting what binds people together: survival during a harsh winter, the common struggle for money, food and shelter. Through such battles we found warmth, friendship and humour. Trust, however, was intermingled with the many strings the church pulled. They wouldn't even admit how powerful they were; they saw themselves as God's messengers, exercising power without responsibility.

There was a car accident in front of our place one warm afternoon. Three of the Dolton brothers, good ol' boys, had been down to the lake to cool off. Not to swim or play, just to sit, fully dressed, in the water, at the same secluded spot just down from our house where we often went skinny-dipping.

As the Dolton boys drove home in their old pick-up truck, travelling in the opposite direction, and fast, was the young neighbour girl. She was known to tear down our gravel road like she had a death wish. There was a loud crash. I ran out.

The three Dolton boys were okay. The girl obviously had a broken leg, probable back injuries, and several cuts to her face and arms. I stopped the bleeding and called for Mary Ann to call for the ambulance.

The oldest Dolton boy said, 'No, call Daddy. He'll know what to do.'

I said, 'Call the ambulance—now.'

The boy yelled again, 'Call Daddy!'

It took a while for the ambulance to arrive. By the time it did, the youngest Dolton boy had already run home and got his daddy.

Mr Dolton was also the local preacher. I'd met him when we'd first moved in to Polaski County. He and his deacon had knocked on our door to welcome us and to say a prayer.

I'd told them that I didn't want them to say a prayer in my house. I'd thanked them and offered them a beer. I think it was only Christian love that prevented them from exploding in rage: there was a definite colour change in their faces.

Preacher Dolton went on to tell us about the close Christian community we'd moved into, and that he was also the local volunteer fire marshal. He explained that if we didn't even want to bother attending the local church, then if our house caught on fire why should they bother to come and put it out?

'Why, no, Sir,' he said. 'We would not feel obliged. And I'd like to say a prayer before we leave.'

And I said, 'No, Sir,' with equally clear distinction.

All of that ran through my mind as I supported the girl's damaged leg in an effort to ease her pain.

When Mr Dolton arrived, the first thing he said was that there was no need to report this to the police; that he would make sure everything would be all right.

Then the ambulance arrived, at the same time as the girl's father. He was a very hard-looking man. Before checking on his daughter he checked the skid marks on the road, then said to Mr Dolton, 'I'll see you in court.' Then he asked me if I'd moved his daughter at all.

Luckily I'd known better than to move her, because of an experience I'd had out on Highway 27 a few months earlier. At that accident the state trooper had said that even though the boy trapped in the upturned car might have burnt to death, if anyone pulled him out and hurt his back he could sue them for everything they owned, and put them in jail.

Time to move on

Even though we had a great place—a big A-frame house on Lake Cumberland—the wages were poor, and it would have taken us a few generations before we could be called locals. So, what with one thing and another, we decided it was time to take a deep breath and move away from the country life, and we put our house on the market.

Atlanta, Georgia, sounded good. One of the drawbacks of living out by the lake was the cost of fuel to get to town. And with the recent jump in fuel costs, living out at the lake was getting very expensive.

One day two guys who weren't locals came down the road and said they thought they might be lost. They said they were looking for some land that was for sale. I said, 'Do you mind if there's a house on it?' They said, 'No,' and eventually they bought our house.

We had lived there for over two years, but saying goodbye was uneventful. Colby's babysitter said the most: 'Well, you weren't never from these parts anyway, were you?' And we drove off.

Atlanta, Georgia, was a modern multicultural town where there was more going on than just religious revivals and deer hunting. It was a move that I hoped would bring happiness and a rekindled sense of awareness, freedom of thought, new challenges and a decent wage. I could feel it in my face, and my step had a spring in it again.

I loaded up our small yellow Datsun for the trip to Atlanta. Mary Ann and Colby stayed at our house by the lake while I drove off with a sandwich and a thermos, looking for work and somewhere to live with a brighter future.

My first day in Atlanta was successful: I scored two jobs.

One was a top-paying job as a journeyman refrigeration mechanic with Earl at Jones Refrigeration. However, it was winter, and Earl said he wanted to employ me but didn't want to put anyone on until spring, so please keep in touch.

The other job was with Coastal States. I was thankful to be starting at any job, as I was out of money. In fact, on the last two days of my first week I would have gone hungry if it hadn't been for the generosity of the head mechanic at Coastal States, Paul, who invited me to stay at his place. He was a Mormon, and I can tell you those people really know how to eat. I'll always have a soft spot for Mormons.

Having some sort of base, even if only for a couple of days, made life so much easier. I was able to look for a house and clean up the back of my van before the boss could see that I'd been living in it.

On Friday night I headed back to Mary Ann and Colby, and to pack up our belongings to be back in Atlanta to start work on Monday morning.

We finished loading the truck on Sunday morning. The truck we had ordered was much bigger than we'd intended, so after loading our meagre possessions we found there was room to fit the car in as well. So 'us'ns', under three-year-old Colby's directions, drove the car up into the truck and the three of us, assuming a bold front, headed off for a new adventure.

We were so confident that things would work out, failure never crossed our minds.

Dennis, Dewey and the big man

During my second week of employment, the president of the company introduced himself as Dennis Dillard, and asked me to fill out an employee information file. One of the first questions was about military service. I wrote down that I'd done two years' National Service in the Australian Army, with active service in Vietnam. When he read that I'd served in Vietnam, he reintroduced himself with a grin—'Captain Dillard, at your service!'—and with a slap on the back, he took me out to lunch.

After lunch we went back to the office, where Dennis introduced me to the office staff. They comprised two secretaries and seven salesmen, two of whom were veterans. Then he showed me around the workshop and talked about the company.

In the workshop there were seven refrigeration mechanics, all young white guys, and five labourers, or 'offsiders', all of whom were black—except for an ex-con who was the company owner's estranged English nephew. Dennis said he would find me a good offsider to work with on my big jobs.

We went back up to the office, where he introduced me to the owner, 'Major' Dewey Thomas, another Vietnam veteran.

It was almost knock-off time when we went back down to the workshop. Captain Dillard gathered everyone around and made sure that I had met all the mechanics. He then said that Ike would be my offsider.

Ike and I shook hands, and Ike laughed. I didn't know why. I said, 'How you doing?', and he laughed some more. His whole body shook up and down with spontaneous laughter as he said to me, 'What you say?'

I said, 'How do you do?'

He said, 'What it is?'

One of the other black guys behind him, who I hadn't been introduced to, said, without looking up, 'What it is, is what it was.'

Ike was a big strong older-looking man. From that first handshake I knew I would like him; anyone who can laugh like that must be all right.

We started working together the next day.

At times he tried to enlighten me, telling me about the dark history of Atlanta and the underground city where people used to hide. He pointed out the Varsity cafeteria and said, 'We do the work in there. It used to be a "whites only" university, and the surrounding streets are where the police set their vicious dogs on the civil rights protesters.'

The Martin Luther King Swimming Pool was one of Ike's favourite places to take a lunch break. He a big man who stood out in a crowd, and it was delightful to see how many people knew him there and how comfortable he looked in the water. The pool was modern, bright and well run. Everyone was comfortable there; even the two white guys with beards and peace signs around their necks. The pool made a bold statement. Even Mayor Brown, with his black entourage, could be seen there.

Ike and I had a horse-and-rider kind of respect for each other. We took it in turns being the rider. I was patient with him and he was patient with me, and out of consideration for each other, a friendship began showing its early light. Ike, sensing the moment, said we could never become real friends because of our cultural differences: there had been too much water under the bridge. His straight talking and honesty made me like him all the more. He was a man who talked without malice, with a smile and a laugh that were uncontrollable.

On the odd occasions when I beat him at his game of throwing quarters to a brick wall—where the one whose quarter ends up closest to the wall picks up all the quarters—he would get slightly annoyed and say you can't beat a black man at his own game. The fact that I was paid three times as much as him made me feel a little uncomfortable when I won. I tried to be generous whenever I could. If we stopped for a beer I would pick up the tab, and lunch went on my company credit card.

Ike and I spent a lot of time driving around Georgia. 'You're all right,' he said to me once. 'Maybe one day I'll take you to a special place. If I do, you might get an understanding of being black. As far as I know, if I do take you—and I probably will—then you might just be the first white man to know where the medal is.'

'What medal?'

But Ike just looked the other way, like he had seen something out the window.

The Chattahoochee

The year was 1981, and over the past two years there had been twenty-three black children, aged between nine and fifteen, murdered under similar circumstances and dumped in the Chattahoochee River.

The FBI was eventually called in, but for months they couldn't catch who was doing the killing. Then one morning at 2 am, during a stake-out at the James Jackson Parkway Bridge, the FBI and the state police, desperate for a breakthrough, heard a splash, and off they went and caught that person.

Wayne Bertram Williams was arrested. He said he was dumping rubbish and didn't know nothing about no murders, but sure enough, forty-eight hours later they found a body just downstream and went to work on DNA evidence. It looked like they had finally got their man.

The murders stopped for a spell. It was obvious to all who read the papers that Williams was the murderer. Everybody hoped that that would be the end of it, even though Williams was a young black man from a good family, with no prior convictions, whose schoolteacher parents were well respected in the neighbourhood. The excuse he gave—that he was dumping rubbish off a bridge at two o'clock in the morning—was never going to hold up in court, especially when a body was found nearby two days later.

Williams not only had known the kid whose body was

found, he'd been seen talking to him the night he went missing. The DNA test wasn't one hundred per cent conclusive but it was enough to satisfy the eight black and four white jurors, and two life sentences were handed out.

One day while we were driving down Ponce De Leon Avenue, Ike made a bit of a statement.

'In 1490,' he said, 'Juan Ponce De Leon was a Spanish soldier fighting Muslims in Southern Spain. Then in 1493 he sailed with Christopher Columbus on his second trip to the USA. Not long after that, Ponce De Leon discovered the Gulf Stream current in the Atlantic Ocean; apparently he'd been searching for the fountain of youth. Later he was badly wounded fighting Indians in Florida, and used that Gulf Stream to escape to Cuba. But it didn't help, because not long after arriving in Havana he died of his wounds.'

Ike would sometimes think up a whole lot of stuff to say at one time, and when he'd finished he would change the subject. It took as much patience as it takes to train a thoroughbred horse to get to the bottom of what he was talking about.

'I really don't understand it,' Ike said to me one day. 'Why a well-to-do black man would go around killing other black men. I don't understand it—especially when two of the victims were mentally handicapped. It just doesn't make no good sense.

'You know where all them bodies are being found?' he continued. 'Well, there was a time when a lot of black people were seen floating in that river.' He pointed down the road. 'If you follow Ponce De Leon going east-north-east, you come to Scott Boulevard. Then follow that to the Interstate 285 ring road and get off at the James E Billy McKinney Highway, and where that crosses the Chattahoochee—that's where the KKK used to have meetings. There's no telling how many bodies that part of the river has digested. The Chattahoochee has many a sad tale.'

Ike did not carry the conversation any further.

Our next service call was on Peach Tree Avenue. We travelled without talking for some time, and then Ike said, 'One day I'll show you where the medal is, and it just might help you understand.'

We carried on for a few more miles, then Ike asked, 'White Australia—you still have that?'

I was uncomfortable and couldn't answer straight away.

'Well, do you have a White Australia policy?' he repeated. I was the horse, and he was geeing me up. I didn't like it, but I thought it was fair.

I said no, but I wasn't sure that I was being completely truthful. 'Perhaps officially we don't,' I said, 'but like anywhere else in the world there are race problems. Just like you said once before about friendship and being from different cultures—we can't pretend that we're the same.'

I told him I hoped our friendship would not be hindered by taking in too much consideration of our race. He laughed at my awkward use of words and said, 'I think I've got you on the hop.'

KKK

I had a birthday party coming up, and I asked Ike if he would come. He shook his head, saying, 'That would be a white man's party; a black man's got no place at a white man's party.'

The last job we had for the day was in what Ike called 'white man's country' on the north side of town. It was a job I had advised on during the installation and commissioning stage a few weeks earlier.

As we drove to the job, Ike looked increasingly uneasy as the colour of the other highway users around us became predominantly white. We had a couple of beers on the way, but when we got there Ike decided to stay in the van.

The job was for a company that specialised in frozen juice concentrates, like concentrated orange and lemon juice. They trucked their products all over the country.

Frozen juice concentrate is an American tradition, just like turkey at Thanksgiving. You need frozen lemon juice concentrate to make whisky sours, and who doesn't want 'fresh' orange juice made from frozen concentrate at breakfast when it's winter and all you can see outside is snow?

The electrician who was in charge of the massive walk-in freezer wanted the temperature brought down to minus forty degrees Celsius. I told him that since he had chosen not to insulate underneath the concrete floor, as we had recommended he do when the freezer was built, he would have to wait until the frost level rose, since ice is a better insulator than earth or cement in preventing heat transference.

He wasn't the smartest electrician I've ever met, that's for sure, and there was no explaining to him that he also didn't need it to be brought down to forty below. All the same, he was very friendly, and we talked for quite a while.

He asked if I was from Australia, and then with a smile he said something about the White Australia policy. He seemed like a great guy, and was easy to talk to.

Then out of the blue, he said, 'There's a KKK meeting tonight—would you like to come?'

I was speechless for a moment, and then he carried on with, 'They do a lot of good—they look after the old people, and if you get injured or sick they'll be the first ones there to lend a helping hand. They even paid for one guy's funeral when he accidently shot himself during a meeting.'

I said, 'Hang on a sec—I'll go and talk to my partner, who's outside in the van, and see if he'd like to come as well.'

'Terrific,' he said.

I went out to my van and told Ike that we'd been invited to a KKK meeting. We both walked back into the building and confronted the sparky, who was now red-faced and retreating backwards towards his office. The closer Big Ike got, the faster that guy moved to the safety of his office with its locked door.

'What do you reckon, Ike?' I said.

'Well, we could kill him, but then we'd have to bury the bastard,' Ike said with a smile.

I said, 'We could make that walk-in freezer real cold, like he wants, and put him in there and lock the door, and by tomorrow morning he'll be brittle and will fall over and be shattered.'

We drove back to the city. Ike offered to buy the beer.

Not much was said for the first few miles, and then Ike said, 'You're all right, for a whitey.'

Then: 'Did you know Atlanta is fifty-seven per cent black?'

I said, 'I know that; I live in a black neighbourhood.'

The rest of the trip was full of idle chatter, encouraged by a beer or two.

I dropped Ike off at our office and said, 'See you in the morning,' then drove home to my place. I was glad we'd moved to Atlanta.

The medal

The next day Ike looked stressed as he lifted his huge body into the van and said, 'Another body was found yesterday. That makes twenty. I don't understand how someone can get killed on such a beautiful day.'

I said, 'It happens like that. I've seen it before. One minute everything is fine and dandy, and the next minute it's not so fine and dandy.'

Ike looked suspicious and said, 'Where did you see such a thing?'

'I was in the Australian Army in Vietnam,' I said.

'I lost a brother in Viet—' Ike was unable to finish his sentence.

Then, anxious and almost desperate to change the subject, he quickly went on: 'My other brother, Tyrone, lived on the second floor of an apartment building, and one day when he came home from work he went up the only stairway to the path that ran all the way around the complex. An angry-looking man was sitting on the path, leaning back against the wall with his legs stretched out to the guard rail. My brother said, "Excuse me," and went to step over the man. The man said, "Go around." Tyrone said, "I just live there," pointing to his apartment. The angry man produced a gun as my brother stepped over him. It was the last step he ever took.'

We had a bit of a drive to our next job, and Ike said he'd show me a shortcut. We turned off the main road to a sandy track that ran alongside the Chattahoochee. It turned out to be a beautiful winding track that was only two or three feet higher than the river, with lots of sandy little beaches. Ike told me that he'd once lived not far from there, and that he'd spent his childhood down on the river. I said, 'You remind me of Uncle Remus.' Ike shook up and down with laughter, and said, 'Now I'm going to show you that special place. You might feel something when we get there.'

We drove along the river, which looks as old as the world, and at one particular bend I pulled up and turned off the motor. There was a rope swing hanging from a tree, a sandy beach, and silence except for the river.

I got out, and Ike said, 'You found it.'

He continued: 'Do you remember when Cassius Clay won gold at the 1960 Rome Olympics?'

'Sure,' I said.

'Well, after the Olympics he left his hometown of Louisville, Kentucky, and was travelling around doing some speaking engagements. One night he went to a classy restaurant with some friends, and they were refused service because they were black. Rumour has it that he was so upset he threw his gold medal into the Ohio River. That's what he said, too, but it wasn't true. He wasn't going to tell all them people up there where he threw his medal.

'It might have been Cincinnati where he was refused service—I don't doubt that—but that's not where he threw the medal, no Sir.

'Next day, Cassius Clay came down here to the Chattahoochee, right here on this very road, and at this very spot. Tyrone saw him get out of his fancy car with his medal around his neck, remove the sash and throw the medal right out there in the middle of the river. For us that know, this is a sacred place.'

A year had gone by and my wages had increased to nine dollars an hour, but Ike was still getting the same meagre wage. I was uncomfortable that my friend had very little chance of improving his lot in life.

We were friends, so I tried to help. I asked Captain Dillard to give Ike some more responsibility, as he could do basic refrigeration work and was a fast learner. He could be trusted, and would take good care of a vehicle.

'He's black,' he said.

'He's a good worker,' I said.

'You don't understand. He's black.'

Earl from Jones Refrigeration had been calling me up every few weeks, asking me to join his prestigious company as a journeyman refrigeration mechanic. The money was fantastic—sixteen dollars an hour—and there was an expense account, plus options to buy shares, and three weeks' annual holidays after the first two years. I had to take it—I knew that—but I felt like I was being swallowed up by the exuberance of the offer.

I said, 'I would love to work for you, Earl, but first I want to take one week's holiday.'

He said, 'Well, Ted, okay then.'

Journeyman

A board meeting of the local union was convened to interview me to see if I was suitable to join the union and thus become a journeyman.

I was marched into a well-appointed room adorned with old-looking paintings and statues. Twelve men sat at a long dark brass-inlaid table. I stood at one end, and they took turns asking me questions.

When it became apparent that I knew more about refrigeration than they did, they started asking me questions about my political beliefs. Did I believe in socialised medicine? Had I ever been a member of a communist party? It took me a few minutes to realise that it wasn't a joke.

When they started asking me about my family in Atlanta, and then about my relatives back in Australia—where they worked, and what their political and religious beliefs were—my skin started to get itchy like I was going to be in a fight.

It was the questions about my parents that pushed the limits of my patience. My fingers twitched and my skin felt warm and ready. It was a feeling I'd had before, when all shit is about to break loose.

The convenor, sensing the tension, got up and offered me a chair, and explained how important it was that they knew their members. The liberties they were taking with their questions were necessary to find out if I could become one of them. He stressed that being a member of their union was a privilege that was rarely offered. He said that if one journeyman refrigeration mechanic was unemployed, they would not allow a new mechanic to join. They looked after their members, he said.

The interview finished a little earlier than I expected, with the convener saying he would write to Jones Refrigeration and let them know their decision.

A week later, Earl from Jones Refrigeration called me on the phone and said that I had been unsuccessful. He sounded a bit angry when he told me that he wanted me to start work in the morning anyway, and that he would arrange a second interview with the union.

The union did not respond to Earl's request for a second interview, and after waiting two weeks he told me not to worry, that I was permanently employed and if the union didn't like it, well, they had just better start liking it. One of the other mechanics told me that legally the union can't ask about your religion or who you vote for.

I enjoyed working with these guys. They were secure, confident and good at what they did.

I quickly made friends. Thomas was a navy veteran who I sometimes met with for a quiet drink and a chat. He had been a signalman on a cruiser serving off Vietnam, and he thought they might have shelled our position during the time when I would have been there.

I told him that I was on the radio one night when a threat like that came in. We were doing some land clearing in Long Hai, thirty kilometres north-east of Vung Tau, when we heard a message to headquarters over the two-way radio from a US cruiser that thought they were under attack from our location and had asked for an area clearance to blow the shit out of our location.

What had happened, I told Thomas, was that the ARVN were having a night practice shoot just down the track from where we were, and their targets were set up in front of the sand hills overlooking the ocean. The problem was that when the recruits overfired the sand hills, their bullets—including the traces—headed out to sea for a mile or so. A passing Yank cruiser, eager for a fight, thought they were under attack, and wanted to return fire.

Our APC crew was parked for the night. The fifty-cal gunner had cleaned his machinegun, the track driver had tied two ends of his tent to the top of the APC and was rolling out his sleeping bag, when the officer in charge of the land clearing ran over from his tent and yelled that we were about to be shelled by a Yank cruiser.

The experienced track driver didn't wait for orders—he yelled to load up, and within seconds he and his gunner were screaming down the sandy track towards the rifle range. The tent flapped behind them as they went over the first sand hill, Mick the gunner screaming that he'd just finished cleaning the fucking gun.

Two or three minutes later we heard the fifty-cal give a short burst. They had driven between the sand hills and the recruits, who must have been shitting themselves. It certainly put a stop to the night firing exercise.

Mick told me later that if the Yank ship had fired on us then it would have been 'Good night, Irene'. We had no protection from the shells the Yank cruisers used. One of the most damaging weapons was the six-inch variable-time anti-personnel. Those bombs have pre-set detonating timers that are initiated once the bomb is fired, so wherever that bomb is when the timer runs out, that's where it explodes. In this case the timer would have been set to detonate at forty feet above our location, thus inflicting the greatest personnel damage.

When two vets get together over a drink, a bond is recognisable and talk is easy. We see each other as we saw each other all those years ago, and our skin is smooth once again. Thinking back to our first days as soldiers, sailors or airmen, we all remember being told the difference between ourselves and civilians. We were no longer civilians; civilians were the other people.

On occasions, Thomas and I would have a sit-down lunch at a Pizza Hut if we were working in the same area. We shared several interests: Australian Rules football, Morse code, pizza, beer and an open mind.

My accent was too much for some passersby; they would have to come over and ask where I was from.

'Australia.'

'You're from Australia? Well, mighty pleased to meet you! I knew some Aussies in Vietnam. Waiter, give this man a beer. You guys are okay.'

I would say, 'I knew some of your guys in Vietnam, too.'

'You're an Australian Vietnam veteran to boot? Well, Lordy, Lordy—have another beer!'

The mechanics got paid sixteen dollars and thirty-four cents an hour, and were guaranteed a forty-hour week. Union dues were two dollars and thirty-four cents an hour, so every week, each mechanic paid a minimum of ninety-three dollars and sixty cents to the union.

When the union board heard that Earl wasn't too happy

with their decision not to grant me journeyman classification, and that he was considering pulling the whole company out of the union, they quickly convened a new meeting. That meeting was informal, and I was treated like a brother, offered a beer and given a contract to sign, as well as a key to the recreation room and a folder full of documents.

When I got home to Mary Ann and Colby that night, we studied the contents of the folder. We'd had no idea how powerful the union was and what being a member entailed. The documents said that for the rest of my life I would be a journeyman. The union would control my wages and would pay my annual three weeks' vacation pay. If I needed a lawyer they would supply one, and when I died they would pay for my funeral. They had their own 'heavies' that I could call on if anyone was causing me grief. It went on and on. They were proud of the fact that no member had ever requested a termination contract—leastways, not for themselves.

Be cool, man

During the great Atlanta snowstorm of January 1982, the city was in turmoil. With no ploughs or salt trucks, there was little the council could do. Well-intentioned pedestrians who might never have seen similar conditions were trying to direct traffic. They stopped vehicles that had just gotten up enough speed to get up a hill to let other traffic cross. Once the cars going up the hill lost their momentum, they would slide back down—staying on the road if they were lucky—until they got to the bottom of the hill to try again.

I was not far from home, heading for the freeway to do a country job, when the snow became a problem. I crossed over the I-75 freeway and saw that no one was moving down there, so I opted to head home, dodging those well-intentioned pedestrians.

It's funny how when something happens—like when there's a major weather event, or someone gets blown up, or you see someone die—disciplined people stand together. Things have happened or are happening that are out of our control, and we need to hold steady. It's only while we are in control that we are of any use, and being of use provides its own protection. Breathe slowly, react slowly, and the warmth of our skin will protect us. When we are required to move fast, then we will move quickly to the betterment of the situation. Panic is never an option.

By the time I got home, the snow on the road had compacted to ice. Mary Ann's car was safely off to the side, and there were lights on in the house.

When I got inside, Mary Ann explained that she had attempted to pick up Colby from preschool with our two-month-old second son, William, strapped in his car seat in the back of our little old car, when she realised it was too dangerous to be on the roads. It was that slippery that when she turned around to come back home she found she was unable even to drive up our driveway.

She had then called the school and spoken to Colby's teacher, who luckily lived just up the road from us and offered to drive Colby home. He'd said he didn't know how long it would take, as he would have a car full of other five-year-olds that he was also driving home, and to keep an eye open for his orange station wagon.

Mary Ann and I reassured each other that everything would be all right, breathed slowly and waited—there wasn't anything else we could do.

At 7 pm an orange station wagon pulled into our street and Mary Ann, with a release of stored-up energy, ran outside to meet the car.

Colby was safe, and asked what all the fuss was about.

'It's only snow,' he said.

Earl called that night and said to postpone the country job, as all the highways were closed and would be for several days. The TV news reported that people were leaving their cars on the freeway, walking to the nearest building with lights on and asking for protection from the storm. Several days later the news reported that many friendships had been made that night, when colour took a back seat and we were all reduced to being human.

Old Gus

Gus was a wise old black man who'd got bored with retirement and asked Earl if he could come back to work. He said he didn't need much money, and he was sure he could help out in the warehouse.

One dark stormy day in spring, we were refitting an old supermarket in Smyrna. One of the things that was constantly in our way was a big old steel safe sitting on the concrete floor. Try as we might, six men couldn't budge the thing.

Gus said, 'Why don't you all go to lunch, and I'll have the thing moved by the time you get back.'

No one took much notice of old Gus, but it was lunch time anyway, so off we went.

When we got back the safe had been moved out of the way, and Gus was sitting down having a sandwich. He refused to tell us how he'd got it moved.

(Some months later, he told me that steel on concrete doesn't slide very well, so what he'd had to do was to go down to the hardware store and buy some six-inch nails. He'd hammered a row of nails horizontally in between the safe and the concrete floor, so the safe was now lying on a row of nails. He'd then laid more nails in a path in the direction he wanted the safe to go. Finally, with a rope and two pulleys, he'd moved the safe by rolling it along the path of nails.)

David

There was a fellow who worked with us named David, who I had known in Kentucky. After his army service he hadn't been able to settle back in to Ohio, so he'd moved to California with a bunch of hippies. A few years later he'd left California in an old yellow school bus in a second wave of hippies heading back east to the Appalachians to buy land and grow vegetables.

I knew David was into smoking dope, but I didn't realise how messed up he was. He'd been a door gunner in Vietnam, and had survived several times being shot down and fourteen times having to make a forced landing. When he moved to Atlanta and asked me if I could get him a job, I said, 'Sure,' as one does for a fellow veteran.

I don't think it was the drugs that made him the way he was. He relived Vietnam every day. One of his nightmares was about when he was shot down and crashed, landing upside-down in a rice paddy. With zero visibility, he'd had grave concerns that his eyes had been damaged, but it turned out that he was in dark water; his harness wouldn't release, and with only seconds left to live he'd cut his way out and made it to the surface. Every day since then he had carried a ten-inch bowie knife.

Thomas didn't like David, nor did Gus, and Earl wondered why I had asked to have him employed in the first place.

Thomas didn't like him because he was from north of the Mason–Dixon line and, like many Southerners, Thomas didn't trust Yankees.

Gus wouldn't say why he didn't like him, but he did say that he wasn't going to ride in the same truck as him, especially if David was driving.

Earl pulled me into his office one day and told me to keep an eye on David. He said there had been a few country jobs where David had put in expense receipts that didn't add up, and that he had also insulted both of the women who worked in the office.

I started to get a bad feeling about David, so I warned him that I would have him sacked if he screwed up again. Sure enough, he soon lost all control, doing one silly thing after another. So that was the end of David, his ten-inch bowie knife and his eyes that opened so wide it was a wonder they didn't fall out.

It wasn't his fault. He was screwed up by the war.

Homesickness

The good thing about doing country work was finding the best motel and the best restaurant in town—but that novelty didn't last more than a few days. The bad thing was that you were an out-of-towner with no family. The accommodation and the restaurants were superficial. No matter how comfortable the bed or how good the food, you were not at home.

Three of us were fitting out a supermarket near Augusta, Georgia. The job would take several weeks, and we had booked three rooms at the Cotton Patch Motel. It had a four-star restaurant and bar, and each room had two king-size beds, a steam-room, box-office TV and room service.

The job took an extra week to finish, which overlapped with the time the US Masters golf tournament was on. It was the big event of the year, and accommodation was booked out for a hundred miles in every direction, but we were able to stay on in our fine accommodation because one of the owners of the supermarket was also a part-owner of the Cotton Patch.

After work we would sit on the veranda, sipping mint juleps and watching the sun set over the pool, while a stream of cars ignoring the 'Full' sign on the road would come in looking for accommodation. Some of the drivers were so tired after watching the golf all day that they would sleep in their cars.

I felt a bit funny about the unfairness. We were living in luxury, with spare king-size beds, while they were sleeping in the car park in their Cadillacs and their Rolls-Royces. But Thomas said not to give it another thought, that the shoe was finally on the other foot.

It was about that time that I started to get homesick. We had been in the USA for nearly five years, and I realised that I was missing the Australian way of life and irreverent humour, where national pride, politics and religion all take a back seat when a joke is at hand.

The many places I have visited—in Asia, Europe and the USA—have all had vastly different senses of humour. Some laugh at fart cushions, some laugh when a goat is born, some laugh when an unpopular senator falls over in a three-legged race. I don't think the humour is better or worse in any particular country, but I do think understanding a new sense of humour is more difficult than learning a new language.

I sent off copies of my resume to refrigeration companies in Sydney and Melbourne, and received several offers of employment. In August we packed all our belongings into seven boxes and shipped them to Melbourne. Then the four of us, with two suitcases in the boot of our little yellow Datsun, headed off to Cincinnati to say goodbye to our American family.

I think Mary Ann's four brothers and three sisters, plus her Mom and Dad, found our departure to a place that was rarely spoken about locally a bit hard to understand. People immigrate to the USA and, if they're lucky, get to stay permanently. But here we were heading off to the other side of the world, with their grandsons in tow.

All the same, they were supportive and spoke positively about our move, and promised they would all come Down Under to visit us.

Danny, Mary Ann's oldest brother, who likes to go for a bit of a drive, said he would like to drive us to San Francisco.

Because our little old car was such a little old car, he said, he thought it would be better if he drove us to the other side of the country. So that's what happened.

We drove for three long days, spent a few great days with old friends in San Francisco and then boarded the big Qantas jet plane that would fly us home to Australia.

For the first few months back in Australia, I felt like a foreigner. I spoke differently and I expected different responses. I went into a bar and asked for a six-pack of the local beer. The barman said, 'We don't sell six-packs,' and another guy at the bar said, while looking the other way, 'He must be a Yank.'

Having spent the past five years in the USA, where there was seldom any news from the outside, I had little idea about Australian politics or what was happening in sport. I began to understand what it must be like to be a new citizen.

In the end we settled back in to multicultural Melbourne, with family and friends and good job opportunities. To top it off, I was able to catch up with some old army mates. In many respects they were philosophically different from me, but our army bond overrode everything, and I was glad to be back on home turf. Then I got the refrigeration contract for Flemington Racecourse, and not only did I get to see four Melbourne Cups, but I got to see them from any vantage point on the course I wanted.

Four years later we moved back to Perth.

Mrs Buj

One person who was really happy about my return was Joe's mum. Joe was working in Canada then, so I often called in to make sure Mrs Buj was all right. She and I had become close friends over the years—ever since my army days, when I'd stayed at her place for a while. We'd shared a few stories that we probably hadn't shared with anyone else. She understood me like mothers understand their sons.

Mrs Buj—Kazimiera ('commands peace')—was fourteen years old when, on her way home from school, the German SS grabbed her off the street of her Polish village. She was taken away and put to work as a servant, cooking and cleaning in a hotel full of German officers. While she was there she saw an older girl who had just turned sixteen shot dead when she refused the advances of a German officer. The girl's last words were, 'I would rather have sex with a dog.'

In the hotel, which was full of happy Germans eating and drinking, Kazimiera learned how to steal and hide food. At night she bravely snuck out of the hotel to give the food to people who were hungry.

Towards the end of the war the Germans were run out of town by the Russians. It was at that time that her brother was shot and killed because he refused to take off his Saint Christopher medal. She never saw any member of her family again.

When the war was over, the only family she had was a baby boy called Jerzy. His father moved to the USA and was never heard from again. Mrs Buj migrated to Australia, remarried and had one more son, Raymond.

Her hatred for Germans continued until late in life, when she finally found herself on speaking terms with a German woman. Mrs Buj told me of this breakthrough, but always referred to the woman as 'the Kraut'.

What it is isn't what it was

I think it's true what my mother said, that 'What's in your head is you, and no one can change that.'

The day after I got discharged from the army I was in a strange space. It was as if I was wearing white clothes, holding a bat and standing in the middle of a cricket pitch during football season. This predicament was similarly described in many of the stories other veterans have shared with me. With time these distortions do subside, and most of us have now found ways to fit in.

As a self-employed refrigeration mechanic I enjoyed the challenges and the peace of mind that came with the solitude of working on my own. But years later, as I settle in to retirement, I have discovered a stronger desire to be similar to everyone else, and to be accepted and be comfortable. No longer do I want to just smile a blank sort of smile and hope no one notices.

This new challenge was not as hard as I thought it would be, and I now look forward each week to golf, the gym, writing, cooking, dieting, brewing beer and having arguments with feral cats. I find myself at peace with the world, and the only challenges I face now are keeping fit and healthy and staying together with my close-knit family around me, along with my friends and my army mates.

Life is pretty good.

Glossary

APC	armoured personnel carrier
ARVN	Army of the Republic of Vietnam
blackboy	an Australian native plant with a long flowering spike rising from its centre, so named because early European settlers thought it resembled an Aboriginal man holding a spear; now more commonly known as grass tree or xanthorrhoea
blackfella	an Aboriginal person
boozer	a bar, or anywhere 'booze' (alcohol) is sold
Coolgardie safe	a rudimentary refrigerator made from a wooden frame with wet hessian sides that cool its contents; named after the Western Australian town where it was first used
donger	a penis
dunny	a toilet
esky	a portable cooler for carrying cold drinks, etc.
in-country	on tour in Vietnam
jackaroo	a young male farmhand
jarrah	a tree native to south-western Australia

karri	a tree native to south-western Australia
KKK	Ku Klux Klan
medevac	medical evacuation
nappies	diapers
RAAF	Royal Australian Air Force
R&R	rest and recreation
roo	kangaroo
roo bar	a metal frame on the front of a car to protect it in the event of a collision with a kangaroo or other wildlife; bull bar
RPG	rocket-propelled grenade
RSL	Returned Services League of Australia
sheila	a woman
sparky	an electrician
stubbie	a beer bottle
TA	tradesman's assistant
texta	a felt-tipped marker pen
VC	Viet Cong
WA	Western Australia
whitefella	a non-Aboriginal person
willy wagtail	an Australian native bird

The eighteenth green

Before I head for the clubhouse I would like to say that these stories are true as best I can remember, and it has been a pleasure for me to write them.

I would firstly like to thank my wife, Mary Ann, for her loving care all through our married life and for the help she has given me in preparing this manuscript; Colby for his help on the computer and his positive thoughts; Will for spelling and reasoning; and our kelpie, Henry, who kept me company regardless of the noises I made.

My special thanks go to Georgia for believing in me as a writer and for the diligent work of Georgia, Leila, Carolyn and Genevieve in guiding this book to publication. For those people who've read my manuscript along the way and offered me support and encouragement I'd like to thank Margot, Mick, Jo Ann, Naama, Rosalie, Ian, Karen and the Rose Book Club, my sisters Bet, Trish and Sue, and my mate Joe Bujnowsk.

I will always be grateful that I am member of a loyal, loving, trustworthy family that has stood by my side through many stressful situations, post-traumatic stress among them. I am indeed a lucky man, in fine company.

The Vietnam War had many consequences. Some of the returned boys had it worse than others, and some still struggle today. I don't know of any veteran who just put the war behind them when they got home and got on with growing up like a normal man. Some of the families of returned soldiers I know unfortunately took a long time to understand this.

My Vietnam veteran gym mates and I get together twice a week for a workout—well, we try. After our strenuous time at the gym we go to Jack and Kelly's, a lovely family-run coffee shop. The fact that they're Vietnamese adds to the enjoyment, as we try to remember things that happened when we were young men. I now understand my father's and his mates' stories that I heard while hiding behind the couch all those years ago.

I sometimes think about people who have died—those I have loved and those I wish I had known better.

www.ingramcontent.com/pod-product-compliance
Lightning Source LLC
Chambersburg PA
CBHW032034290426
44110CB00012B/796